The
Transformed
Kitchen

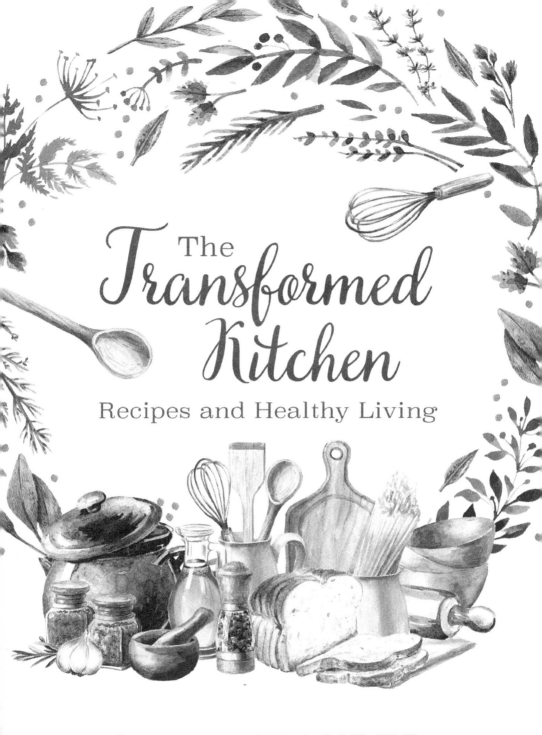

The Transformed Kitchen

Recipes and Healthy Living

LORI ALEXANDER

author of *The Power of a Transformed Wife*

Forward

My mom was raised in a church that believed that drugs, doctors, and demons were synonymous. She then married a doctor! When I was five years old, she was diagnosed with ulcerative colitis. The doctors told her that there was no cure. She went the medical route of drugs for a while but grew sicker. She gave up and decided to find a natural cure. For five years through trial and error, she was pronounced cured after a colonoscopy.

She began feeding us mostly organic food after this. We would travel a half hour to a health food store to have lunch and load up on organic food for a week. I loved doing this with my mom! She was considered a "health nut" long before eating healthy became popular.

Many women today feed their family as culture dictates. They don't read ingredients and fix what's easy and their family likes. Health problems have skyrocketed. Cancer, heart disease, and diabetes are the ones of rich nations that have ballooned since seed oils were introduced on the market. Seed oils are soaked in Hexane which is a petroleum product. Petroleum is NOT a food!

When I was growing up, I don't remember anyone being allergic to our cats or peanut butter. Now, it's an epidemic! Obesity in children is rising. Autoimmune diseases are becoming commonplace. Women need to learn how to care for their families and help make them as healthy as possible. Also, drugs don't heal. They're toxic to the human body and should only be used in emergency situations.

We must be as wise as serpents, women, and learn to take good care of our families. I have had many years of health issues; thus, I had a lot of time to research good food and natural remedies. In this book, I will share my time-tested family favorite recipes and all of the natural healing ways that I have learned along the way. I don't have a lot of recipes. I cook and feed my family simply, but learning from me, you will be able to expand, in many ways, meals that are healthier for your family.

This may all appear completely overwhelming to many of you at first. It may all be something brand new for you. I encourage you to not feel you need to do everything at once. Begin with baby steps and do what you can do. I address this in more detail at the conclusion of this book.

Women, you have a huge influence on your family and their health. You are the homemaker in your home! Begin choosing food the way God created it to be eaten over fast and convenient food that is filled with harmful ingredients and causes devastating diseases. This takes time and effort, but it is all well worth it! After all, the kitchen is the heart of the home.

Table Of Contents

Bread Recipes

SOURDOUGH EINKORN BREAD

Einkorn is far healthier than regular wheat because most wheat in America is heavily sprayed with glyphosate-containing (RoundUp) which destroys the gut. "Health begins and ends in the gut," claimed Hippocrates, the father of modern medicine. Einkorn is the only wheat that is completely unhybridized. My son-in-law is sensitive to wheat and has fairly severe reactions from it. He tolerates this Einkorn flour well. Fermenting it even makes it far easier to digest. I have baked with Einkorn flour now for many years and use it in all of the recipes calling for wheat in the same measurements. Einkorn is the purest and most ancient form of wheat available. ("The Healthy Home Economist" has a great post about this flour.)

My sister gave me my first starter. You can try making your own. I never have, or you can buy one on Amazon. You don't have to keep your starter out and feed it every day. You can put a tight lid on it, then put it into the fridge for two to three weeks. Feed it, then keep it out for a day before using. If you're not going to use it yet, then put it back to sleep in the fridge. It's very easy! (I've gone up to three weeks but it's probably best to feed it every two weeks. If you're gone for a long time, simply freeze it.)

In preparation for making the bread, feed the starter 1/4 cup organic white flour and 1/4 cup filtered water, then mix. Cover with a cloth and keep on the counter overnight.

Now, you will make the levain. Find a small jar and pour in 25 grams of the starter, then 75 grams organic white flour and 75 grams of filtered water. Stir well with a spoon. Cover with a small cloth and set in the oven with the light on for four or more hours until the levain rises. Make sure it has risen a lot! This is key to fluffy bread.

Here is the scale that I use: OXO Good Grips 11 Pound

Food Scale with Pull-Out Display, Stainless Steel. You need one that can measure a large load! I have made the mistake of buying one that was too small, and it made it far more difficult to measure out in portions.

After the levain has risen, take a large glass bowl and pour in 700 grams of water, add the levain and mix well with a dough whisk. Add 800 grams of Einkorn white flour, 200 grams of Einkorn whole wheat flour, and 30 grams of salt. (You can use all white Einkorn flour too.) Mix well with a dough whisk and then cover with saran plastic wrap or a large plate. Leave overnight and even into the next day depending on how well it has risen. In the cooler months, I wrap it in a blanket.

I buy my Einkorn flour at Vitacost.com when it is 20 percent off. Sign up for the emails and watch for the sales. I buy it in 10-pound bags.

Here is the name of the dough whisk that works great: Danish Dough Whisk Blender Dutch Bread Whisk Hook. You can buy proofing baskets on Amazon or just use large bowls for when the dough is divided and rising.

The next day, put some Einkorn white flour on a smooth counter and take the dough out of the bowl using a spatula. Pour flour on top of the dough and then separate it into two loaves using a dough divider. I use one called ALLTOP Bench Scraper & Chopper for Kitchen, Stainless Steel Pastry/ Dough/Food Cutter Tool. Work one piece of dough at a time as shown on my YouTube channel on how to make this bread (fold the top side of the circle of dough to the bottom, then rotate the circle a little bit and again fold the top side to the bottom again and again 50 times), then place in a proofing basket that has a cotton cloth (some of the baskets come with a cover, or you can use kitchen towels) after pouring some rice flour on the cloth so the dough won't stick. Do the same with the second piece of dough. Cover them with a towel.

Keep baskets on the counter for one or two hours and then in the fridge for one or two hours. Preheat the oven to 500 degrees with the Dutch Oven in it. Make sure the oven is very hot before putting the bread in it. Take the Dutch Oven out of the oven and dump the bread into the Dutch Oven with heavy oven mitts. Put the lid on and place the Dutch Oven back into the oven for 20 minutes. Then lower the oven to 465 degrees, take the lid off, and cook it for 10 more minutes. Take the bread out, dump it onto a bread-board to cool, and preheat the oven back up to 500 degrees to cook the second loaf.

After it has cooled, I will usually freeze one loaf but cut up the other one and freeze it. You won't have to freeze the loaves but can keep them on the counter in a Ziploc bag if you have a family who will eat it in a few days. Cut it up as you use it. It keeps it fresher this way.

This bread makes GREAT French toast, and grilled cheese, tuna, and turkey sandwiches. You can use it for anything that you would use regular bread for. It's great with a lot of butter soon after it comes out of the oven. Nothing tastes better than fresh bread right out of the oven!

WHOLE WHEAT BREAD

I have been making this bread for many years now, and I've never ruined it! My husband refuses to eat any other kind of bread. It is delicious! I will try to make the directions as clear as possible. Here it goes:

This makes 5 loaves. (I have a video of making this on my YouTube channel.)

Heat up 6 cups of water to 110 to 120 degrees in a pan on the stove.

Pour water into a Bosch Mixer which is by far my favorite or use a KitchenAid which you will probably have to cut the recipe in half.

Add:

   2/3 cup of honey

   2/3 cups extra virgin olive oil or avocado oil

   2 Tablespoons of sea salt

Start mixing and slowly add 5-8 cups of freshly milled whole wheat flour or sprouted spelt flour. I grind my own wheat berries with a Wondermill grinder, but you can also buy whole wheat flour. (If you have a problem with wheat or gluten, you can try sprouted spelt flour or even Einkorn flour. My daughter makes this with spelt flour for her husband who is gluten intolerant, and it's wonderful! You can buy it at health food stores.) You need to use hard wheat berries or regular whole wheat flour NOT soft wheat berries if you want to grind your own wheat.

Sprinkle 2 tablespoons of SAF yeast over it and mix well. I use the yeast that comes in the big white package from Costco and store it in the freezer. Let the dough sit for 20 minutes. It will begin to bubble and rise.

Then start adding flour one cup at a time while the mixer is on and keep adding flour until the dough just begins to clean off the sides of your bowl and gather together, then begin the kneading time. You will be using about 18 cups of flour total but you may have a half to one cup left over. Instead of all whole wheat flour, I add two cups of millet to it, and you can add oatmeal or other flours also. The total shouldn't be more than 18 cups however. Too much flour makes the bread too crumbly and dry. My daughter has even added oregano, basil, onion and garlic powder to it to have an Italian flair. It's really good!

Knead the dough for about 5 to 7 minutes. Your dough should be soft, slightly sticky, and the sides of the bowl shouldn't have much dough clinging to it. So, add some more flour if it is too sticky.

Afterwards, divide the dough into 5 parts (just eyeball it) and shape into a loaf and put into well-oiled bread pans. I use a little bit of liquid lecithin (found in any health food store) and olive oil to coat the pans, and they never stick.

Preheat the oven to 170 degrees, turn the oven OFF, then put the bread in the oven. Let it rise for 30 minutes.

After 30 minutes, turn the oven to 350 degrees with the loaves still in the oven and cook for 35 minutes. Take the bread out and use a knife or spatula to pop them out of the pans, then let them cool on a cooling rack. You can slice them up and put them in the freezer after you've let them cool off completely if you want the bread to last longer.

"And Jesus said unto them, I am the bread of life: he that cometh to me shall never hunger; and he that believeth on me shall never thirst." (John 6:35)

Breakfast
Recipes

EINKORN STARTER PANCAKES

Here's a great recipe to use for the sourdough starter you won't be using. My grandchildren love these pancakes!

In one bowl, mix together:

> 2 cups Einkorn flour
>
> 2 teaspoons baking powder
>
> 1 teaspoon baking soda
>
> 1 teaspoon salt
>
> 2 tablespoons coconut sugar

In another bowl, whisk together:

> 1 cup sourdough starter
>
> 1 1/2 cups coconut milk (You can use organic milk IF you have no problems with dairy.)
>
> 2 large eggs
>
> 2 tablespoons melted butter
>
> 1 teaspoon vanilla

Add all of the ingredients together by gentle folding. This recipe makes ten good sized pancakes.

I put ghee on a hot cast iron skillet and cook them on this. Then I put butter and real maple syrup on them. These will be the most delicious pancakes you've ever tasted! My husband requested an egg on top of his. I will never throw away any of my starter ever again.

Every good gift and every perfect gift is from above, and cometh down from the Father of lights, with whom is no variableness, neither shadow of turning.

JAMES 1:17

HOMEMADE KEFIR

Kefir is FABULOUS for your gut!!! A healthy gut is imperative for a healthy immune system, and it's full of good protein. It tastes a lot like yogurt but regular yogurt only has around five different probiotics, whereas kefir has over thirteen! I make my own and it is very easy.

Buy a gallon of organic, whole milk.

Pour into a large pan on the stove and heat to a slow, rolling boil, stirring frequently.

Let cool to room temperature.

Add 1 cup of organic store-bought kefir to it and stir well.

(After the first batch, you will save a cup from this batch for the next batch and so on.)

Pour into quart size mason jars.

Put in the oven with the light on or in a dark cupboard.

Cover with a light towel.

Let it sit for at least 8 hours. Check after 8 hours and see if it is thick like yogurt. If it is separating, you have it in too warm of a place or have left it too long. If I put it in the oven, it takes 6 to 8 hours. If I put it in the cupboard, I can leave it overnight.

Cover with lids and put it in the refrigerator. It lasts up to three weeks. Just use as you would regular yogurt. Save one cup of your homemade kefir for your next batch. Eat a half of a cup or more a day for good gut health.

KEFIR SMOOTHIES

These are great for your children to begin their day with!

In a blender add:

> 1 cup homemade kefir
>
> Several cups of organic frozen fruit
>
> One or two frozen ripe bananas

Blend until smooth. My grandchildren love these!

KEFIR-SOAKED GRANOLA

Soaking grains makes them easier to digest and better for you. Cooking it at such a low temperature also makes it healthier.

Put into a large bowl:

> 8 cups rolled oats
>
> 1 stick melted butter
>
> 1/2 cup melted coconut oil
>
> 1 1/2 cup kefir or yogurt

Stir well. Put a towel over it and let it sit for 24 hours.

Heat in a small pan on low just until warm:

> 1 1/2 teaspoon vanilla extract
>
> 1 1/2 teaspoon almond extract
>
> 3/4 cup raw honey
>
> 1 teaspoon sea salt
>
> 1 cup unsweetened coconut

Mix everything together along with:

> 2 1/2 teaspoon cinnamon
>
> 1/2 cup dates pieces
>
> 1/2 cup almonds
>
> 1/2 cup walnuts

Spread on two large cookie sheets and bake at 170 degrees for as long as you want. I baked them for four hours, and the granola was chewy. If you want it crispy, you will have to bake it for a lot longer. I eat my granola with fruit and kefir for a healthy breakfast.

FRESH LEMONADE

Babies are born very alkaline. They have pretty pink tongues. Breastfed babies keep pretty pink tongues. Formula fed babies get a white coating on their tongues. They become more acidic. When you die, you are very acidic. Disease breeds in acidic bodies. Therefore, the key is to stay as alkaline as possible.

There are lists out there of alkaline and acidic foods. The foods that God created are more alkaline. All processed foods with sugar and seed oils are acidic. So, eat as many alkaline foods as possible to keep a strong immune system.

Some ways I make sure I get plenty of alkaline food into my body is to have a big glass of warm herbal tea first thing in the morning. I put in a teaspoon of good sea salt, the juice of a whole lemon, and a teaspoon of raw, organic honey in it. Your body has been fasting overnight, and this is a good thing to start off with; NOT coffee which is very acidic and hard on your adrenals. Coffee is a drug, and all drugs have side effects. Anything that is addictive can have side effects.

After workouts or after you sweat a lot, instead of Gatorade which is full of junk, try the juice of one whole lemon or limes, sparkling or regular water, a dash of good air-dried sea salt (to restore electrolytes and minerals), stevia, and ice. It tastes similar to Gatorade but is much tastier and better for you!

I also make sure I have a big salad every day with all kinds of greens and vegetables of all different colors with some protein and healthy fats in it. For snacks, give your children fruit and properly prepared nuts and seeds. I have jars of pistachios, sunflower and pumpkin seeds, almonds, walnuts and cashews on the top shelf in my refrigerator. Fruit and nuts were my children's favorite snack growing up. Grass fed beef sticks are good too. Give them healthy food growing up, so they will have a taste for it when they are adults. If you live in a climate that supports lemon trees, grow them. I have a few lemon trees and love picking lemons off of them for my morning tea.

I know some mothers are unable to nurse their babies and dislike the idea of giving their baby formula. My grandma bought a goat and gave one of her baby's raw goat's milk. A goat only grows up to be around 150 pounds, just like human beings so the protein is similar to human milk. Cow's milk is way too concentrated. Cows grow up to be a ton. Soy is full of estrogen which is not good for babies, especially boy babies.

So, study nutrition. Being healthy along with a strong and healthy immune system are wonderful gifts you can give your children. It is a lot cheaper than being ill in the long run. My mom raised us on organic food way before it was popular. Most cancers and diseases can be prevented. I met a woman in a Bible study who was in severe, constant pain as a result of chemotherapy and radiation. She lived on morphine. She told me she was so sorry she went the chemotherapy route. It just wasn't worth it. Live to prevent cancer and other diseases.

"He causes vegetation to grow for the cattle and all that the earth produces for man to cultivate, that he may bring forth food out of the earth." (Psalm 104:14)

BANANA BREAD

This makes one loaf. I found the most popular banana bread recipe on Google and then changed all of the unhealthy ingredients like white flour and sugar and used Einkorn flour and coconut sugar instead. I also add an extra egg for added protein and nutrition. My husband loves nuts in it too, so I added them.

Ingredients:

    2 to 3 medium overripe bananas, peeled and mashed

    1/3 cup melted butter

    1/2 teaspoon baking soda

    1 pinch salt

    3/4 cup coconut sugar

    2 large beaten eggs

    1 teaspoon vanilla extract

    1 1/2 cups Einkorn flour

Preheat the oven to 350 degrees.

Mash bananas and mix in melted butter in a bowl.

Mix in the beaten eggs and vanilla, then add the rest of the ingredients together in another bowl and mix thoroughly with the wet ingredients. I add a cup of chopped walnuts too. Pour into a well-buttered bread pan.

Bake for 55 to 65 minutes until the knife comes out clean.

PUMPKIN BREAD

I did the same thing when my husband asked for pumpkin bread. I turn an unhealthy recipe into a healthy one. You can do this with everything you cook and bake, women!

My husband's favorite food is pizza, so I now make him an Einkorn crust and homemade sauce. He loves it!

This recipe makes two loaves.

Ingredients:

- 1 15 oz. can organic pumpkin puree
- 4 large eggs
- 1 cup melted butter
- 2/3 cup coconut milk
- 3 cups coconut sugar
- 3 ½ cups Einkorn flour
- 2 tsp. baking soda
- 1 1/2 teaspoon salt
- 1 teaspoon cinnamon
- 1 teaspoon nutmeg
- 1 teaspoon cloves
- 1/2 teaspoon ground ginger
- 1 cup chopped walnuts

Mix the wet ingredients together in a bowl, then mix the dry ingredients in another bowl. Add them together and stir well. Pour into two well-buttered bread pans and cook for 50 minutes at 350 degrees until the knife comes out clean.

ALMOND CRUNCH COFFEE CAKE

This is definitely a crowd pleaser, plus it is healthy. I actually don't make anything that isn't, because I believe the purpose of eating is to nourish our body. In order for your car to run well, you need to give it good gas. In order for you to run well, you need to give it good food. Even people who don't like healthy food like this!

Preheat the oven to 350 degrees.

Almond Topping:

Blend until crumbly

> 1/4 cup Einkorn flour
>
> 4 Tablespoons organic coconut sugar
>
> 3 Tablespoon melted butter

Stir in 1 cup chopped almonds

In a separate bowl:

Blend thoroughly

> 3 eggs
>
> 3/4 cup honey
>
> 1 teaspoon vanilla

Mix in 1 cup buttermilk (or 1 cup milk or coconut milk with 1 teaspoon lemon juice)

Blend in separate bowl:

> 2 cups Einkorn flour
>
> 1/2 cup coconut sugar
>
> 2 teaspoons cinnamon
>
> 1 teaspoon baking powder
>
> 1 teaspoon soda
>
> 1/2 teaspoon salt
>
> 1/4 teaspoon ginger

Blend dry ingredients into liquid ingredients until smooth.

Pour into a greased 9" X 13" pan. Top evenly with almond topping.

Bake for about 30 minutes until the knife comes out clean.

SOAKED, SALTED, AND DEHYDRATED NUTS

These are so good! Soaking nuts (our favorites are almonds, cashews, and walnuts) in salt water makes them far more digestible. I buy raw, organic nuts from the bins at the health food store. Costco even sells them now!

Take 4 cups of nuts and cover them completely with good, filtered water.

Add one to two tablespoons of good, air-dried sea salt. (Redmond's is my favorite!) It depends on how salty you like food. I like mine salty.

Let them soak overnight. The exception is cashews which should only soak for six hours, or they will not work.

Spread them out on cookie sheets and put them in your oven or dehydrator on the lowest setting for several days until they are nice and crunchy. (It may take only a few hours in an oven depending upon how low it cooks them.) I use these nuts for many of the things I bake and make!

These nuts make a great and healthy snack.

Dinner
Recipes

*W*omen have asked me for a menu plan. I have never had a menu plan. I ask my husband what he wants for dinner, then make sure I have all of the ingredients and make it for him. I shop once a week at my health food store. I go to Costco a few times a month. We have one a few miles away. I am not a gourmet cook, and I don't have a ton of recipes. I stick to the ones my family loves! Some of you may want more variety. Recently, my husband wanted a pot roast, so I searched Google for the most popular recipe and made it for him. He loved it!

ROASTED CHICKEN

Buy an organic, whole chicken.

Put into a casserole type of pot or Dutch oven to cook in.

Cover the chicken with avocado oil and salt liberally.

Put in a whole cut up onion and lots of garlic bulbs.

I like to put in a big sprig of rosemary from my garden.

Put the lid on and cook at 300 degrees for two hours.

Take the lid off and cook at 350 degrees for another half an hour.

Take out of the oven, cover, and let sit for about 10 minutes before eating.

CHICKEN BROTH

Take all of the chicken meat off of the roasted chicken.

Leave everything else in the pan: the bones, fat, and skin.

Fill the pot with water.

Cook on the stove for three to five hours.

When it's cool, pour it through a strainer into a clean bowl.

Put the broth into mason jars, and you can freeze it if you aren't using it soon. (Leave at least an inch or so at the top if you are freezing it to give room for it to expand and not break the glass.)

Use this as a base for all of your soups and stews. It makes them so healthy and delicious!

HEALING VEGETABLE CHICKEN SOUP

This soup is great for the winters and times where sickness is going around. It's easy to digest and full of healthy, healing ingredients.

Take a whole onion and chop it up.

Sauté in butter and ghee for about 15 minutes. Salt well too.

Add some garlic and sauté for a short time.

Add the homemade chicken broth with a tablespoon of both dried oregano and basil.

Then add lots of potatoes, yams, carrots, green beans, peas, and whatever other vegetables you love in soup.

Cook on low until the potatoes and yams are cooked, then cut up the chicken and add it to the soup.

Salt and pepper to taste.

Homemade broth is so good for the entire gut!

SPICY CHICKEN CURRY STEW

My husband loves curry! He was raised in the Caribbean where they eat lots of curry. This has been a family favorite for many years. I still make it often in the cooler months.

In a large pan:

 Melt 4 Tablespoons of butter

 Add 1 large chopped onion

 Add 1 1/2 cups each of carrots and celery

 Add 1 Tablespoon minced garlic

 Sauté for 15 or so minutes.

Then add:

 1/2 teaspoons each of ginger and cumin

 2 teaspoons of salt

 2 teaspoons of curry powder

 1 cup of lentils (brown or pink)

Then you can either add four uncooked chicken breasts with the skin on, or add the chicken from the roasted chicken in at the end. This is what I do!

Add:

 6 cups of homemade chicken broth

 1 cup of brown or white rice

Bring to a boil, turn to simmer, and cook for an hour. Then take out the chicken, throw away the skin, and cut it into bite sized pieces if you put in four uncooked chicken breasts. Now, start tasting it and add more seasonings until you love it! If a soup ever tastes too salty, add a peeled and chopped potato to it and it will take away the saltiness.

CASSI'S SALAD DRESSING

My daughter created this dressing many years ago and now people around the world are enjoying it! People have told me they love it so much that they could drink it. It helps those who aren't fans of salad to enjoy eating them.

In a blender, add:

> 2 egg yolks (I only buy organic, pastured ones and
> have never had a problem with them.)
>
> 4 teaspoons sea salt
>
> 1 teaspoon pepper
>
> 4 teaspoons Dijon mustard
>
> 2 minced garlic cloves
>
> 1 cup balsamic vinegar

Blend thoroughly and then pour in 1 cup of extra virgin olive oil and 2 cups of avocado oil while the blender is going. Don't over blend! This will last in the refrigerator for about three weeks.

MY NUTRITIOUS SALAD

I have a big salad almost every day for lunch. I chop up romaine, red leaf lettuce, and arugula then wash it all in my salad spinner.

Clean and chop up radicchio, celery, carrots, red peppers, and whatever other vegetables you love in salad.

I top my salad with sauerkraut, avocado, pumpkin seeds or walnuts, chicken, sardines, turkey, or steak for protein, tomatoes, and salad dressing. It's highly nutritious and delicious! (If I could eat cheese, I would definitely put that on it too.)

HELPING CHILDREN LIKE VEGETABLES

Cut up a lot of vegetables like cucumbers, red peppers, and carrots in bite-sized pieces. Children seem to like these.

Use Cassi's salad dressing for a dip. Most children love this!

Concerning picky eaters, I didn't allow my children to be picky eaters. They ate what was set before them. If they didn't like something, they had to eat a few bites unless it was something like salad. They had to like salad in my home! They all love salads as adults. If they only ate a small portion of their meal, I would leave it there for when they were hungry. They couldn't have anything else until they finished most of it. I wanted my children to like healthy food. Thankfully, they all do!

A friend of mine married a widow with several children. These children did not like vegetables! She loves salads, so she would eat them often. The children eventually wanted to taste her salad. Recently, she told me that the children ate a salad! She was so excited. Model to your children healthy eating. Say, "Yum, yum" while you are eating it. Let them see that eating healthy can taste good too!

"I have no greater joy than to hear that my children walk in truth." (3 John 1:4)

PIZZA CRUST AND PIZZA SAUCE

My husband loves pizza, but most pizzas are not healthy. It's filled with seed oils, white flour, and ingredients that don't nourish a body. I went on a quest to make my husband a pizza that was healthy and that he loved. He LOVES this one! Top it with all of your favorite foods. My husband loves green pepper, mushrooms, tomatoes, broccoli, pepperoni, bacon, sausage, mozzarella and cheddar cheese.

PIZZA CRUST

Get a small glass bowl and with a wooden spoon, mix together:

- 1 cup Einkorn flour
- 2 teaspoons yeast
- 1 1/2 teaspoon coconut sugar
- 1 teaspoon salt

Heat up water and add 2 Tablespoons of extra virgin olive oil and 3/4 cups of warm water. Mix thoroughly.

Add 1 1/3 cup more flour and stir well. Cover with a plate, put it in the oven with the light on, and allow it to rise for 30 minutes.

On a well-oiled (extra virgin olive oil) pizza stone, either use your fingers to press the dough out or a rolling pin. It's crumbly so I have found just using my fingers is easier.

Put into an oven that has been heated to 425 degrees and cook for 10 minutes.

PIZZA SAUCE

Mix these ingredients together, and that's it!

- 6 ounce can tomato paste
- 15 ounce can tomato sauce
- 2 tablespoons dried oregano
- 2 tablespoons Italian seasoning
- 1/2 teaspoon garlic powder
- 1/2 teaspoon onion powder
- 1/2 Tablespoon onion powder
- 1/2 Tablespoon garlic salt
- 1/4 teaspoon black pepper

After you cook the crust for 10 minutes and put the sauce on the crust, top with all of your favorite toppings and put into an oven heated to 425 degrees and cook for 10 minutes.

CHICKEN OR BEEF TACOS

This is one of my most requested meals by my youngest son. It's a great meal to make for company or a large gathering too!

I roast two chickens or fry some organic ground beef in my cast iron skillet.

I buy organic, sprouted taco shells from my health food store. Most corn is GMO, so I won't use it unless it's organic. You can also make or use whole wheat tortillas.

Make some black beans from scratch or buy a few cans of them.

Sauté some onions until caramelized.

Make some homemade guacamole or cut up some avocado.

Make some homemade salsa, buy some, or cut up some tomatoes.

Make some Spanish rice. My son loves this on his tacos! (Find the most popular one on Google, and make that one.)

When everything is ready to serve, heat the tortillas for 15 seconds on both sides in ghee or avocado oil in a hot iron cast skillet. Then have your family or guests fill up their taco shells with anything they want and top with cheese.

CHILI AND BLACK BEAN SOUP

I have been making this soup for many years, and it is still our family's favorite. A friend of ours from church brought it to us the night before we moved into the home we presently live in. It was a huge blessing! Chili Powder and cloves give it a wonderful flavor.

In a large pan:

Heat 2 Tablespoons of avocado oil and 2 Tablespoons of butter, then sauté 1 large, chopped up onion.

After 10 minutes, add 2 cloves of minced garlic.

Sauté several more minutes.

Add:

> 4 cups of chopped up, uncooked chicken breast or chicken from the roasted chicken at the end
>
> 4 cups or 2 cans of black beans (I sometimes make black beans from scratch.)
>
> 3 cups chicken broth (Homemade Chicken Broth)
>
> 1/2 cup uncooked brown or white rice
>
> 2 T. fresh cilantro (if you have it)
>
> 1 T. dried basil (fresh if you want)
>
> 1 1/2 teaspoons chili powder
>
> 1/4 teaspoon cloves

Bring to a boil. Turn to low. Cover and cook for 1 hour. After 1 hour, slowly add more of the seasonings (salt, chili powder, cloves) IF it needs it. (Mine usually doesn't.) That is the secret to good soup. Add some cayenne pepper to it if you like it spicy!

THANKSGIVING GRAVY AND MASHED POTATOES

This is a great gravy for those who are sensitive to wheat and corn (most corn is GMO). Put 1/4 cup of butter into a pan and melt the butter. Add in 4 cups of homemade chicken broth. Shake in a glass jar 1/4 cup arrowroot powder with a little bit of cold broth. Slowly add it to the pan while whisking until it is thick and creamy. Then add salt and pepper to taste. It is thick and delicious!

For the mashed potatoes, use Yukon potatoes and scrub them clean without peeling or cutting them. Put them into a big pan with cold water. Salt the water, then bring it to a boil and simmer until the potatoes are done. Strain out the water, and my husband uses a potato masher to mash them, skin and all! I add a cup of melted butter while he mashes them. Then add salt and pepper. They're excellent too!

We make this Thanksgiving Day feast simple. My son-in-law smokes the turkey. I make the gravy, mashed potatoes, and pies. I bake some yams too. I did buy some cranberry sauce at the health food store but this was it, and everyone was completely satisfied! I love simple and delicious food. (My son-in-law would maybe admit that the entire turkey thing wasn't that simple!)

"This is the day which the LORD hath made; we will rejoice and be glad in it." (Psalm 118:24)

THYME LEMON CHICKEN THIGHS

This is a simple, yummy dinner. With two whole lemons cut up, onions caramelized, and big chunks of garlic, your family is sure to love this dish!

Ingredients:

   8 to 10 red potatoes

   8 thighs or chicken legs with bones and skin

   1 large sliced onion

   6 garlic cloves peeled and smashed

3 large carrots

2 lemons cut into wedges

thyme

salt

pepper

ghee or avocado oil

Since learning that ghee is the best fat to cook things in, I melt several tablespoons of it in my large cast iron skillet. Then put all the chicken pieces in the pan, salt and pepper them, and cook each side for about 8 minutes.

Remove the chicken from the pan and put the onion in the same pan, salt, and cook until slightly caramelized, about 10 minutes. Add garlic and cook for another 5 minutes.

Put potatoes, carrots, onions, and garlic into a large baking dish with a lid. Salt and pepper and then lay chicken pieces on top. Sprinkle liberally with thyme. Put in the 2 cut up lemon wedges in between the chicken pieces. Put into the oven with the lid on.

Cook at 350 degrees for about an hour or until the potatoes are soft. You can take the lid off for the last 15 minutes if you want to brown the chicken up a little.

You have a whole meal in a pan. Enjoy!

SWEET POTATO CHICKEN CHILI

This is a spicy, very easy and filling chili that your family will love!

Sauté in a large pan:

1 Tablespoon ghee or olive oil

1 chopped up onion

4 cloves of garlic minced

After ten minutes add:

2 Tablespoons chili powder

4 teaspoons cumin

1/4 teaspoon salt

2 1/2 cups chicken broth (Homemade is always best!)

2 cans black beans (or make your own)

1 can diced tomatoes

Juice of 1 lime

1/2 cup fresh cilantro

1 large sweet potato chopped up

2 cups chopped up uncooked chicken breasts (or chicken from a roasted chicken)

Bring to a boil, put the lid on, and simmer until the sweet potatoes and chicken are thoroughly cooked.

After serving in bowls, you can top with cheese and tortilla chips if you would like.

CHICKEN ROSEMARY STEW

Preheat oven to 425 degrees

In a cast iron skillet (use any old skillet if you don't have a cast iron one):

Coat the bottom of the pan with ghee, butter, or avocado oil.

Salt and pepper 8 chicken thighs with the skin and bones.

Cook each side in oil for 8 minutes, then remove from the pan.

Sauté 1 chopped up carrot, onion, and 2 pieces of celery in the fat for 10 minutes.

Add 2 sprigs of rosemary. I leave them whole and take them out before serving.

Squeeze 1 lemon into the pan and scrape the bottom of the

pan to get all the yummy stuff off.

Place the chicken on top of all the vegetables.

Add 2 1/2 cup chicken broth (Homemade Chicken Broth)

Bring to a boil.

Put it in the oven for 40 minutes. Put chicken and vegetables over brown rice. Very yummy!

HEARTY CHICKEN PARMESAN

This is an easy dinner to make if you are feeding a crowd. It is definitely my family's and guest's favorite dinner!

In a large pan:

Melt one stick of butter.

Take 6-8 boneless, skinless chicken breasts and cut them into long, narrow strips.

Lay in the chicken on top of the butter.

In blender or Cuisinart add:

  3 slices of whole wheat bread or my homemade bread

  1 cup of Parmesan cheese

  1 teaspoon garlic powder

  1 teaspoon sea salt

  Several stems of parsley or cilantro, if desired

Blend until crumbly.

Spread bread mixture over chicken.

Sprinkle it with paprika.

Bake at 350 degrees for 45 minutes.

If it starts getting too brown, cover with tin foil. I put this on top of my Homemade Spaghetti Sauce and whole wheat pasta with some Parmesan cheese.

CHICKEN, BASIL, KIDNEY BEAN SOUP

Everything I cook is easy and healthy. I am not a gourmet cook. I like things to be simple. I use mostly organic ingredients in all my cooking. This is a simple, healthy stew. It is very filling and good!

In a large pan put:

3 Tablespoons olive oil

2 stalks chopped up celery

3 chopped carrots

1 large chopped onion

Sauté about 10 minutes.

Stir in 2 14-1/2 ounce cans chopped organic tomatoes with their juices

2 14-ounce cans chicken broth. I use my Homemade Chicken Broth.

1 cup fresh basil leaves

2 bay leaves (I have a bay leaf bush in my backyard so I have LOTS of bay leaves!)

1 teaspoon dried thyme leaves

Juice of 1/2 lemon

4 chicken breast with ribs or add some roasted chicken cut up when the stew is done cooking (This is what I do with all my soups since I make so many roasted chickens, and I think chicken tastes best roasted.)

2 15-ounce cans of organic kidney beans, or make your own (Soak 2 cups kidney beans in water overnight. Add 1 Tablespoon of salt. Bring water to boil. Cook on low for an hour. Drain and use for stew.)

1/2 cup organic brown rice or quinoa

Bring to a boil and then simmer for 1 hour, less if using quinoa.

Take the chicken out and shred into bite-sized pieces. Return to stew. Salt and pepper to taste. If you used homemade chicken broth, you won't need as much salt and pepper.

TURKEY, BLACK BEANS, AND BROWN RICE CHILI

This has been a family favorite for years. It is hearty and perfect for a cold winter night!

In a large saucepan:

Sauté 3/4 lb. of ground turkey (or beef) in 1 Tablespoon of avocado oil

When meat is browned, add 1 large, chopped onion.

Cook for 15 minutes.

Add:

- 2 cans (15 oz. each) diced tomatoes
- 2 cans (15 oz. each) black beans
- 2 teaspoon chili powder
- 1 teaspoon cumin
- 1/2 teaspoon sea salt
- 1 Tablespoon sugar

Let simmer on the stove for an hour or put in the crock pot for 4-6 hours uncovered.

Taste after a while and add more of the seasonings until it is seasoned enough for your taste. We like it very well seasoned.

Fix another pan of brown rice and pour the chili over the rice. I sauté the rice in avocado oil until it turns slightly brown then homemade chicken broth instead of water to make it healthier and tastier.

Delicious and filling!

SPAGHETTI SAUCE

This is one of my family's favorites that I have been making for years!

In a large pan:

Brown 2 lbs. of meat (ground turkey or beef) in 2 Tablespoons of avocado oil or ghee

Salt the meat with 1 teaspoon of salt and 1 teaspoon of pepper

Add 1 large, chopped onion and cook 15 minutes

Add several minced cloves of garlic (or more if you love garlic)

Add 25 oz. jar of a marinara or spaghetti sauce

2 14.5-oz. cans of diced tomatoes

1 14.5-oz. can of fire roasted tomatoes

2 Tablespoons dried oregano (or fresh if you have it)

2 Tablespoons dried basil (or a big handful of fresh)

1-2 Tablespoon coconut sugar

pinch of cayenne (ONLY if you want it very spicy!)

Simmer 2-3 hours uncovered. Start tasting and slowly adding more salt, pepper, sugar, and cayenne until it is seasoned to your liking. We use this sauce on whole wheat pasta with fresh Parmesan cheese. I add fresh mushrooms and broccoli to it sometimes for the last 1/2 hour of cooking. You can put it on any type of pasta you like or over brown rice or even slices of zucchini, and it's delicious!

HEALING BONE BROTH

If you have any digestive issues such as ulcerative colitis, Crohn's disease, IBD, IBS, Celiac, allergies, and even things like acne and eczema (all skin issues are a result of a bad gut), I encourage you to watch the video by Jordan Rubin on YouTube called "Ten Keys to Conquer Crohn's and Colitis." His book "Restoring Your Digestive Health" is great too! He completely healed his Crohn's disease even though doctors say there is no cure. I recommend this video, book, and broth to anyone with health issues since health begins and ends in the gut!

Here is his recipe for healing bone broth that he recommends consuming one to two cups three times a day. This is the crucial element in healing gut issues.

3 quarts filtered water

1 tablespoon apple cider vinegar

4-6 tablespoons coconut oil

1 medium organic, free-range whole chicken

8 organic carrots, sliced

6 stalks of organic celery, sliced

2-4 organic zucchinis, sliced

3 medium-size organic white or yellow onions, peeled and diced

4 inches ginger, grated

5 cloves garlic, peeled and diced (omit if you have upper GI problems or severe heartburn)

2 to 4 Tablespoons of sea salt

Place the filtered water in a large stainless steel pot, add the apple cider vinegar, and let stand for 10 minutes. Add the oil, chicken, vegetables, ginger, garlic, and sea salt; and bring to a boil over high heat. Let boil for 60 seconds, then lower the heat and simmer for 12 to 24 hours. About 30 minutes before removing soup from the heat, add the parsley if desired. Remove the soup from the heat. Remove the chicken meat from the bones; place the chicken meat back in the soup and discard the bones. Ladle into soup bowls and serve hot. For acute situations with high inflammation, allow the soup to cool, then puree it in batches in a high-powered blender or food processor. Some people with extremely severe conditions may want to discard the chicken and vegetables and consume only the broth. Consume one to two cups three times daily during the healing phase.

Desserts

PUMPKIN PIE AND CRUST

I have been making this since we were married. My husband loves this pie, so I make it for him throughout the year. You can double the recipe to make a lot more filling in the crust. It just needs to cook longer.

In a blender, add and blend well:

  2 eggs

  1 15 oz. can of organic pumpkin pulp

  3/4 cup maple syrup

  1/2 teaspoon sea salt

  1 teaspoon cinnamon

  1/2 teaspoon ground ginger

  1/8 teaspoon ground cloves

  1/2 cup coconut cream or coconut milk

  1 teaspoon vanilla

Pour into the frozen pie crust or make your own. Put onto a cookie sheet into a 425-degree oven. Cook for 15 minutes. Lower the heat to 350 degrees and cook for 45 more minutes or more. It is done when a knife comes out of it smoothly. I whisk organic heavy whipping cream with added maple syrup and vanilla to go on top! Delicious!

I found out that even the pie crusts in the health food store have seed oils in them so I made my own! It's easy.

  2 cups Einkorn flour

  2 Tablespoons coconut sugar

  1 teaspoon salt

  7 Tablespoons melted butter

  4 Tablespoons of ice water

Mix together. It's crumbly so I have found that just patting it in with my fingers works best.

Pour in the pumpkin filling and then cook it with the pumpkin filling in it.

EMMA'S CHOCOLATE CHIP COOKIE BARS

My oldest granddaughter brought the recipe over to my house and made these for us. Everyone loved them so I have been making them ever since!

Mix in one bowl:

   3 cups Einkorn flour

   1 teaspoon baking soda

   1 teaspoon salt

   1 cup coconut sugar

   A bag or less of healthy chocolate chips

   Mix in another bowl:

   1 cup of melted butter

   1/2 cup of maple syrup

   1 teaspoon of vanilla

   3 beaten eggs

Mix all of the wet and dry ingredients together. The dough is quite wet but spread on a well-buttered cookie sheet with a spatula. I spread it so it's about 1/2 inch deep.

Cook at 375 degrees for 11 minutes. Don't overcook them! They're good and chewy a bit undercooked.

Let them cool, cut them with a spatula, and then store them in a Ziploc bag in the freezer. They won't last long!

HEALTHY CHOCOLATE

Most everyone loves desserts but white, processed sugar is bad for everyone. It is the cause of most diseases and plays havoc on the gut. A healthy gut is needed to be healthy. My sister, Alisa, took an intensive health class that lasted almost a year. She has found great recipes to build up and nourish our bodies instead of tearing them down. Most everyone, however, loves a sweet once in a while so she told me about this chocolate candy recipe that is delicious. Even my grandchildren love it.

Coconut oil is very good for us so I have tried to get it into my diet, and this is the best way I have found. I buy my supplies at Trader Joes, Costco, and online.

Ingredients needed:

1 cup organic coconut oil (Costco's organic brand is great!)

1 cup raw organic cacao powder (Divine Organics)

1/4 cup raw organic honey, maple syrup, or coconut sugar (I've been using 1/2-part Y.S. Organic Bee Farms Raw Honey and 1/2 part Big Tree Farms Brown Coconut Sugar with a small squirt of Now Liquid Organic Stevia)

1/2 cup organic cacao nibs (optional)

1 cup organic peanut butter (Santa Cruz organic is the best) or 1 cup pumpkin seeds (or any mixture of nuts) My favorite is 1/2 cup peanut butter and 1/2 cup properly prepared walnuts.

1 teaspoon vanilla

pinch salt

Melt the coconut oil in a glass bowl over a small pan with simmering water in it. Put everything in the blender and mix it well. It needs a strong blender. Pour on parchment paper or a silpat liner that is on a large cookie sheet and spread it around. Put it in the freezer for an hour or so, then break it off into pieces. Store it in the freezer in a plastic bag, but I doubt it will last long! My grandchildren and everyone who tastes it love it.

"For he satisfies the longing soul, and fills the hungry soul with goodness." (Psalm 107:9)

When I am looking for a new recipe, I google the most popular recipe of what I am looking for and replace the bad ingredients for good! I exchange flour for Einkorn flour, sugar for coconut sugar or maple syrup, one extra egg for added protein, milk for coconut milk (if you have an allergy to milk) and so on. I haven't had one fail me yet!

Healthy Living

THE IMPORTANCE OF SALT

There are three times I should have died due to low sodium. Death levels are below 126. Normal levels are 135 to 145. When I arrived at the hospital all three times, I had a sodium level of 110. A few people in the medical field have told me they have never known anyone who survived a sodium of this low level.

Salt is full of minerals needed for health, NOT the Morton's salt in the grocery store which is highly processed and all of the minerals are stripped from. No, we need good air-dried sea salt the way God created it. I only use Redmond's sea salt now. I even bought a 10 gallon jug of it. I can never run out of salt and neither can you! People have died from drinking too much plain water, because it strips their body of sodium. They pee it all out.

After the third time being in the hospital due to low sodium, the doctors put their heads together and finally figured out what was happening. My brain tumor greatly damaged my pituitary which is the major producer of hormones in the body. It was no longer informing my kidneys to retain water, so I would pee all of my sodium out. Therefore, they told me I was allergic to free water. I can't drink a lot of water. I must take at least two teaspoons of sea salt a day. Since this diagnosis, I have been able to keep my sodium levels up and not have to go to the hospital.

God calls us to be salt and light. Salt is important even to God! What does salt do? It preserves food and makes it taste better, just as we help preserve cultures by our godliness and make it better. Everyone around us should be able to tell that we're different by the way we treat them and live our lives.

*"Ye are the salt of the earth: but if the salt
has lost his savour, wherewith shall it
be salted? it is thenceforth good for nothing, but to be cast out, and to be trodden
under foot of men." (Matthew 5:13)*

*"Let your speech be alway with grace, sea-
soned with salt, that ye may know how ye
ought to answer every man." (Colossians 4:6)*

*"Salt is good: but if the salt has lost its
saltiness, wherewith will ye season it?
Have salt in yourselves, and have peace
one with another." (Mark 9:50)*

GENERAL GUIDELINES FOR HORMONAL HEALTH

Written by my oldest daughter who was infertile for seven years. She researched becoming healthy which in turn helped her to conceive. We are so thankful!

Avoid all artificial, processed and packaged foods and beverages.

Choose organic produce and organic, grass-fed meats when possible.

Aim for 80-120 grams of protein per day.

Eat breakfast (especially before any caffeine). It's best to have protein early in the day and carbohydrates later in the day.

Drink a minimum of half of your body weight in ounces of pure water daily. Add electrolytes once or twice a day. (Sea salt would be good!)

Avoid eating anything other than a light snack of protein and/or fat near bedtime.

Eat large amounts and a variety of brightly colored vegetables daily.

Use healthy organic fats liberally which includes ghee, organic butter, well-sourced tallow or lard, and coconut oil for cooking. Use Olive, avocado, flax, hemp, walnut, sesame oils for dressings. Supplementation with quality balanced essential fatty acids is recommended.

Include plenty of traditional foods such as fermented foods, slowly cooked soup broths made with fish, chicken, or beef bones.

Chew, chew, chew. Eat your meals and snacks in a calm, relaxed state to support digestion, and chew your food well.

Listen to your body. Eat when you are hungry and stop when you are satisfied.

Try to go four to five hours between meals to support blood sugar and give digestion a break. Eating whole, real foods with fat and protein should make you feel more satiated and less prone to snacking. A snack should be small in quantity and only enough to hold you over until your next meal. If you have signs of low blood sugar, eat more frequently but you may also want to investigate if you have underlying anemia or B vitamin deficiency.

If you struggle with infertility and would like help from her, you can reach her at info@fertilitywellnessco.com and her website is www.fertilitywellnessco.com.

THE TRUTH ABOUT SEED OILS

When I was growing up, we were told seed oils like canola,

safflower, and sunflower oils were far healthier than extra virgin olive oil and butter. I guess few decided to research how they were made. It was just something most of us believed. Seed oils are terrible for our health. Here is the process of how they are made:

First, seeds are gathered from the soy, corn, cotton, safflower, and rapeseed plants.

Next, the seeds are heated to extremely high temperatures; this causes the unsaturated fatty acids in the seeds to oxidize, creating byproducts that are harmful to human and animal health.

The seeds are then processed with a petroleum-based solvent, such as hexane, to maximize the amount of oil extracted from them.

Next, industrial seed oil manufacturers use chemicals to deodorize the oils, which have a very off-putting smell once extracted. The deodorization process produces trans fats, which are well known to be quite harmful to human health.

Finally, more chemicals are added to improve the color of the industrial seed oils.

"This process uses bleach, lye, and hexane to transform an inedible product into a low-grade toxin that may not kill you immediately, but which causes long-term health problems. Soybean oil and all other seed oils must be processed in the same industrial manner because of the tiny amount of oil encapsulated in each tough little seed. Only a factory method using volatile chemicals is able to extract enough of that oil to make it lucrative for the extractor.

"Before seed oils came onto the scene, heart attacks were unheard of: cardiologists in the early 20th century never saw them, and any sudden heart failure leading to death was due to a congenital defect. Cancer was rare and so was obesity. Then the captains of industry found out that they could dump their waste onto the food supply through the magic of industrial chemistry—similar to how they dumped fluoride in the water supply—by offering payola to medical associations for a stamp of approval. They also dangled the prospect of future high-paying jobs to government workers as long as they approved their toxins as food." (The article where I found this information can no longer be found.)

There was a video made 10 years ago showing us how seed oils were made, and the video was supposed to teach us how healthy seed oils are for us! This video shows that the seeds take a 70-minute bath in Hexane which is a "significant constituent of gasoline." Seed oils are extremely inflammatory in the human body. They aren't food, and they aren't for human consumption.

Did you know that seed oils are in almost everything? Most chips, cereals, cookies, salad dressings, and everything else are filled with seed oils. Most people are eating a lot of healthy destroying seed oils every day. The healthy fats are butter, tallow, ghee, coconut oil, avocado oil, and extra virgin olive oil. The bad fats are canola, soybean, sunflower, corn, safflower, grapeseed, margarine, cottonseed, and peanut oil. Begin replacing all of the food you eat with food that has healthy fats in it. It's one of the best things you can do to improve the health of your family.

"Beloved, I wish above all things that thou mayest prosper and be in health, even as thy soul prospereth." (3 John 1:2)

DOCTORS AREN'T GOD. DO YOUR OWN RESEARCH.

They wanted to give my husband a pacemaker when he had Lyme Carditis and his heartbeat was at 22. He researched that it took seven days on antibiotics to clear the infection. So, he stayed awake seven days and nights in the ICU with paddles strapped to his bed (if he fell asleep, his heart would stop) and on the seventh day, his heart rate went up!

My close relative had to get a vaccine for work and was up all night very ill. His wife took him to the ER early in the morning. My husband raced down there with his laptop. The doctor said he had appendicitis and needed his appendix out immediately. Ken researched that in Europe they always give antibiotics, and it clears up in a week. The doctor fought them, and my relative had to sign a release. He was better the next day! (A side effect of the vaccine is appendicitis.)

A close friend of mine had numbness and tingling in her feet and hands. She had also suffered from arthritis. She went to doctors and many appointments along with some painful tests for a year. They couldn't figure out what was wrong with her. Her brother was coming to visit in a month. He only eats Keto, so she went to a bookstore and bought a recipe book for the Keto diet. So, for a month, she only ate Keto. Something amazing happened! All of her numbness, tingling, and arthritis were gone! She now mostly eats Keto since she feels so much better on it.

My mom was diagnosed with colitis when I was five. Doctors said there was no cure. She tried the medical route and became sicker. After five years of trial and error of what she could and couldn't eat, she was completely healed! She proved it to the doctors with a colonoscopy.

The neurosurgeon who did my first brain surgery wanted

to get to the tumor by going through my upper lip. Ken had researched that doctors were going through the nose and asked him to do it that way. The doctor had done over 1200 of these surgeries! He said "no" but the night before surgery, he came and looked up my nose and said he would go up my nose! It was an easier recovery (still rough), but I wouldn't have had any feeling in my top teeth if he did it through my lip!

Do your research. It's okay to question doctors. They aren't God. Sometimes, you have to be your own doctor.

"For our light affliction, which is but for a moment, worketh for us a far more exceeding and eternal weight of glory." (2 Corinthians 4:17)

DON'T GAIN WEIGHT BECAUSE YOU'RE GETTING OLDER!

One man wrote this on Twitter: "Don't let your body fat percent increase just because you get older. Charts like this often show healthy range increases with age. In reality, there seems to be no reason for the increase, other than that it's common." Our culture has accepted as fact that people get fat as they age. Why? Because most do, but they shouldn't.

Here are some hints for staying attractive to your husband and not gaining weight as you age:

- Exercise at least one-half hour a day, six days a week. I love to go on walks.
- Eat a light dinner and no eating after dinner. It's far easier if you don't snack between meals too.
- Eat food the way God made it. Cut out all

processed sugar and seed oils.

- Weigh yourself every day or once a week. Nip it in the bud quickly!
- Go to bed early and wake up early.
- Get plenty of fresh air. Leave your windows open as much as possible.
- Don't get angry or worry. Live one day at a time.
- Smile and choose to be joyful.

We do need to eat less as we age. We don't need as much food. Our metabolism and thyroid slow down. We're usually not as active. We still need to do what we can to stay attractive to our husbands, however, plus all of these things make for good health!

I needed to lose a few pounds a few months ago. I wrote a post about it. I later told a friend about it. A week or so later, she asked if she could text me her weight every morning so I could hold her accountable. I have been doing this for her for about three weeks now. Her weight will go up if she cheats. She has a goal before going to Europe soon. I told her no more cheating, so she doesn't. She's close to her goal. Accountability is a good thing!

I do all of those things and have for a long time. I just learned that I can't eat desserts, sweets, and too much bread. Everyone is different. Some can eat more of those things and not gain weight. This is not about being skinny. It's about being the weight that you feel most comfortable with and most healthy. The Apostle Paul told us that he disciplined his body and kept it under control so that he wouldn't be disqualified. He also tells us that we should be known for our temperance (moderation) in everything.

In closing, it's good to be disciplined and self-controlled. Everyone knows this, but for some, it's incredibly difficult.

What are they to do? Have some type of plan and account-ability. Make short goals and keep them. Get rid of all of the junk in your home. Begin making everything from scratch. I rarely eat out. Research sites and learn about health. The Weston A Price Foundation is a good place to start. Remind yourself that you can do all things through Christ who strengthens you, and that a fruit of the Spirit is self-control. With God's help, you can do this!

"But I keep under my body, and bring it into subjection: lest that by any means, when I have preached to others, I myself should be a castaway." (1 Corinthians 9:27)

MY BOUT WITH SHINGLES

Many years ago, my aunt told me that she and a friend both had shingles at the same time. Her friend went the doctor/drugs route, and she went the chiropractor's route which was to take nine L-lysine capsules the first day, eight the next day, and so on. By the ninth day, she was so much better, and her friend was still suffering. I wrote this down, so I would never forget in case I ever contracted it. (This was one of my aunts that was raised by my grandma who believed that drugs, doctors, and demons were synonymous!)

A few years ago, my BIL who is a doctor told me that shingles has exploded since the chicken pox vaccination. "Mass varicella (chicken pox) vaccination is expected to cause a major epidemic of herpes-zoster (shingles), affecting more than 50% of those aged 10–44 years at the introduction of vaccination." Before the chickenpox vaccination, it was unheard of for older people to get shingles. The shingles vaccination also spreads shingles. The makers of the vaccination even admit this to be true! "Transmission of vaccine virus may occur between vaccines and susceptible contacts."

Well, a few Decembers ago, my back began itching. The next day, I looked to see if I had a spider bite, and there was a clump of bumps. I immediately suspected shingles, so I began taking L-lysine.

I remembered that Jacqueline from Deep Roots at Home had written about having shingles, so I carefully read and studied her blog post about it. Some had asked me if I was going to go to the doctor and go on the antivirals. Jacque did that, and it made her shingles so much worse, plus she suffered side effects from the drug. As soon as I knew what it was, I knew I wouldn't go to the doctor. Drugs don't agree with me, and I know that they have a lot of side effects. Drugs, for me, are only for emergency situations.

From her blog, I ordered these homeopathic pellets for nerve pain called Hypericum perforatum 200ck. (I can't take Tylenol or any of those kinds of drugs, because they hurt my stomach.) They definitely took away some of the throbbing nerve pain at night so I could sleep. My fifth day was the worst, and I was taking three of these under my tongue every hour. I also ordered the Shingles Nosode that Jacqueline recommended, and I was taking ten drops a day three times a day until I read that when the condition is acute, take it every 15 minutes for three hours and then once every hour after that. So, I did this. I also used Calendula Cream on my rash which helped with the burning, itching pain a lot. I did take my normal vitamins of C, D, and others every day too.

On the tenth day after the rash broke out, I began feeling much better. It was very painful. I never reached a 10 in pain, but was pretty steady at six and seven between days four through eight. I did put a pack of frozen corn on the throbbing pain behind my shoulder frequently. (The shingles was on my upper back, side, and breast.) Since icing helps dramatically with the nerve pain in my neck, I figured it would help with the nerve pain from shingles. My daughter had shingles many years ago and the only thing that gave her relief were the ice packs. I definitely saw a great improvement by day nine. I was even able to take a small walk around the park!

One thing I have learned through this experience is to do all you can to prevent contracting shingles by taking a capsule of L-lysine every night before bed (It helps with sleep!) and take 10 drops of the Shingles Nosode once a month under your tongue. I will be doing these things from now on to hopefully never catch this again. It is no fun at all. Everything you read about shingles states that the pain can last between three to six weeks, and even longer if you get the post-nerve pain. I didn't want this to happen to me, so I did everything I could to prevent this. It's now several years since I had Shingles, and I have no lingering pain. A friend of mine at church got it about the same time I did when many were receiving the Covid shots. I believe this is how we got it. The shots do shed.

*"The LORD will strengthen him upon the
bed of languishing: thou wilt make all
his bed in his sickness." (Psalm 41:3)*

ALL OF MY NATURAL CURES

On Instagram, I have been teaching women a lot about health. You can't find health in a drug or a shot. It's our responsibility to be as healthy as we can!

My grandmother was raised in a church that believed drugs, doctors, and demons were synonymous as I have shared. When she found out about vaccinations, her response was, "I'm not injecting that poison into my babies' bodies!" She had all seven of her children at home. She never took any of them to the doctor. When they were sick with a cold or flu, she would give them warm water with fresh lemon juice and some honey. She raised them on a lot of fresh fruits and vegetables, raw milk, and the likes. When she couldn't nurse her third baby, she bought a goat and fed the baby raw goat's milk. Goats grow to be about 150 pounds. Cows grow to be 1,200 pounds. Goat's milk is far closer to the composition of human's milk. I had a wise grandmother! She lived well into her nineties. Her daughters all lived into their late 80s and 90s.

My mom married a doctor. When she got Colitis when I was five years old, she tried the medical route which told her there was no cure. She needed to live on white food like white rice and bread, and also take steroids. She only grew sicker. She went to a place where she fasted on water for 21 days, then they gave her fresh vegetable juices. After about six years of trial and error, she was completely healed and even had a colonoscopy to prove this to the doctors. She raised us on organic food and was always trying to find natural cures for everything.

I shared all of this to give you my history, and why I believe the way that I do. Doctors and drugs are FANTASTIC for emergency situations. I would not be alive without them.

I have to take two drugs for the rest of my life to survive, but the drugs don't keep me healthy. They keep me alive. Every year when I meet with my endocrinologist, he asks me if I am experiencing a long list of side effects from these drugs. I do what I can to keep myself healthy, but then depend upon the Lord. He knows the number of my days.

We never vaccinated our children after reading "The Poisoned Needle." We learned that most diseases cleared up with sanitation and clean water. Did you know that shingles has skyrocketed among the younger people since the chicken pox vaccination? It is far more painful than chicken pox ever was. I am not a fan of vaccinations. I trust my immune system more than I do these shots.

Here's my list as far as I can remember everything:

- **UTIs – Clear Tract**. It has cleared up all of my UTIs, even when I had a fever. It works in a day or two. It's amazing! I had a friend who struggled with them for many years and was on many rounds of antibiotics. This stuff cleared them up within a few days! (Sadly, everything has gone up so much in price, since I last bought it due to our government's uncontrolled spending.)

- **Sinus Infections – X-Clear Nasal Spray**. This stuff is amazing! I had never had a sinus infection before my first brain surgery. But since they drilled up through my sinuses, I have struggled with them. This is the only thing that clears them up. Last September, my son and his family were here for three weeks. During this time, pneumonia, fevers, coughs, and strep went around our home. My son and I used X-Clear religiously three times a day in hopes of preventing getting sick. Neither of us did! We were both amazed and thankful. Now,

I use this stuff often, especially after I have been around sick children or out shopping.

- **Gut issues – Repair Vite**. I had undetected parasites for many years. Then, I had to take a ton of powerful drugs to rid my body of them which destroyed my gut. I finally was given this stuff by a Naturopath and found relief. It's very expensive, but it was so worth it to finally have a healthy gut. (This has almost doubled in price since I last bought it. I find it's cheaper if I buy it through a chiropractor or naturopath.)

- **Frozen shoulder or any other type of structural pain – The Trigger Point Therapy Workbook**. This book is amazing! Any time I have any structural pain, this is my go-to book. After my neck fusion, I had such intense pain from my frozen shoulder. This book is written by a cardiologist who found that her heart patients had more pain from frozen shoulders than from their heart surgery. They got it from laying around so much. This happened to me. I began trigger point therapy on it as explained in this book and within a month, I could raise my arm above my head!

- **Headaches – Peppermint essential oil**. Just last night, I woke up with an aching temple, so I put some of this stuff on it. The headache was gone when I woke up! This has helped me numerous times with the many headaches I have gotten from having such a bad neck. It's great stuff! I use the DoTerra brand.

- **Acid Reflux – Betaine HCL and digestive enzymes.** After my first brain surgery, my esophagus and stomach were fried from all of the hydrocortisone they pumped me full of. I took the acid-reducing drugs for a year, but they failed to help at all. I was listening to Dr. Marshall almost every day at that time. He talked about the importance of air-dried sea salt (Redmond's) and HCL to help digest food. He taught that acid reflux was due to a lack of HCL, so the food rots in the colon and the lactic acid from this comes up and damages the stomach and esophagus. I began taking HCL and digest after every meal. I also drank a lot of aloe vera juice. I wish I had known about Repair Vite too, since it has aloe vera and all of the healing ingredients for the gut in it. I eventually healed and now take HCL daily after meals with meat. You must also eat an inflammatory diet until it heals. Don't eat any citrus, vinegar, or anything that can cause burning pain. Eat hours before bedtime so your food is well digested by bedtime.

- **Burns – Fresh Aloe Vera**. One time, my youngest daughter burned her foot badly. I slapped a piece of fresh aloe that I had in my backyard on her foot and changed it throughout the day. Within a week, the skin on her foot was slightly pink and almost healed. It's amazing stuff for any type of burns.

- **Dry eyes – Organic Castor Oil**. After my first brain radiation, I had dry eyes. The radiation had killed my tear ducts. I didn't want to put something artificial in my eyes every day, so I researched it and found that castor oil works great! I put it into my eyes every morning after I wake up.

- **Eczema** - A few of my grandchildren have struggled greatly with this disease. It's terrible! One of my DILs was determined that her fourth baby wouldn't have the same struggle that her last two children had, so she did her research. Her fourth baby has always had beautiful skin and has never struggled with eczema because of what she fed this baby. The book she learned from is called "Super Nutrition For Babies."

- **Pre-skin cancer, warts, and moles – Black Salve**. This is highly controversial, but I have been using this stuff on any sores on my skin that won't heal for over 20 years now, and it's fantastic. I wrote a post about it many years ago on my old blog Always Learning (lorialexander. blogspot.com if you want the details). If you Google it, you will never use it, because they show all types of horror stories with it. I have never experienced any and neither has anyone I have given it to. (It's expensive, but it lasts for many, many years.)

- **Tendonitis – The Tendonitis Expert** (tendonitisexpert.com). This guy saved me so much pain! I have had a bad neck for many years from car accidents and running into a plate glass window. At one point, my neck was so bad that I was in immense pain all of the time. I went to a surgeon and he told me I needed my neck fused. So, I had my neck fused but found no relief at all. I researched what could be causing such intense pain, and I finally found The Tendonitis Expert. I found out that the pain was caused by inflammation, so I needed to ice my neck 20 minutes on and 20 minutes off throughout the day. I used frozen corn packs. I did this every waking moment for a month and was finally able to get out of my recliner! His icing methods have helped me with other injuries too.

- **Sore throat – Gargle with warm salt water often**. Take a few teaspoons of the strongest Manuka honey you can find every day which is GREAT for all types of skin infections too. Sip on warm water with fresh lemon juice and raw honey throughout the day.

- **Gallbladder problems** – My husband was having gallbladder attacks which were extremely painful, but he didn't want to have surgery. He knew he needed his gallbladder to digest fats, so after researching, he went through numerous gallbladder cleanses that had to do with a lot of olive oil and other things. He healed his gallbladder! Research it to find out the various ways to do this.

Any time you find yourself dealing with any health problems, research natural cures for it. This is what I have done for many years. I have found people who have healed themselves from MS, Parkinsons, cancer, etc. A man in our old church was diagnosed with prostate cancer last year and decided to go the natural route before surgery. Jordan Rubin, author of "The Maker's Diet" put him on a strict diet along with intermittent fasting. After about eight months, his cancer was completely gone! Yes, drugs and doctors are fantastic for emergency situations, but not so good for chronic conditions.

"In the midst of the street of it, and on either side of the river, was there the tree of life, which bare twelve manner of fruits, and yielded her fruit every month: and the leaves of the tree were for the healing of the nations." (Revelation 22:2)

MY THOUGHTS ABOUT BIRTH CONTROL

"The issue of birth control cuts to the core of the diabolical disorientation of the family in the Western world. When your daughter, sister, wife, or girlfriend swallows that pill, not only does she ingest all the artificial hormones that increasingly are linked to breast cancer and strokes later in life, she ingests our society's judgment of her worth.

"Birth control is inherently harmful in that it disrupts something that is good and performing according to its nature: fertility in women. But, fundamentally, the pill cancels the primary, unique, and healthy function of the female body. By taking what is objectively good and terminating it, even temporarily, the pill is injurious and ultimately unjust by its very nature.

"For women, for whom fertility is the harbinger of their greatest power (child formation), a cancellation of fertility attacks their very essences and being. In essence, it changes a woman. Birth control is an implicit attack on the beauty of life itself" ("Stop Putting Your Daughters on Birth Control" by Karolina Provokatsiya).

My mother never offered us birth control in high school. She taught us to save ourselves for our future husbands, so we did. We knew our virginity and future ability to have children within the bonds of marriage were something to treasure. We didn't give our daughters birth control but told them to save themselves and taught them the value of being virtuous, so they waited until marriage.

Too many parents aren't teaching their children, so their children wander aimlessly through their teenage years going along with the flow and having many scars to show for it. Many women have told me that their parents never told them anything about waiting for marriage or being virtuous.

For all who want to tell me that they HAVE to take birth control pills, I want to tell you that, no, you don't. The side effects are numerous and all the pill does is mask the symptoms. Go to a Naturopath and get to the root of your problems. Begin cleaning up your diet and eating whole, nourishing foods the way God created them to be eaten. Cut out sugar, junky oils, processed foods, and all of the other things that are health and gut destroying.

The pill can cause young women to be infertile. It can cause them to abort embryos (newly created human beings). It causes many other things and is toxic to the human body. It has led to the slaughtering of millions of unborn babies, because it has made babies disposable, unwanted, and inconveniences.

Stay pure until marriage and then welcome babies into your lives. Yes, they take a lot of time, energy, and patience but the rewards far outweigh the negatives. Never take your fertility for granted, young women. Those women who are infertile can tell you the pain and grief it causes to not be able to bear their own children.

Protect your fertility from a young age by not using any type of birth control, not having sex before marriage, eating healthy (get rid of plastics and anything that is hormone disrupting), and taking care of yourself. You do what is in your ability to do while living in obedience to the Lord, then rest in His providence for your life.

This is from the Natural Nurse Momma on Instagram:

Birth control (synthetic hormones)....

- Causes estrogen dominance and prevents ovulation
- Doubles the risk of candidiasis (yeast)
- Increases sex hormone binding globulin which decreases libido
- Increases lifetime risk of depression if used before age 19
- Depletes B vitamins, magnesium, selenium, Vitamin C and E
- Impairs methylation
- Alters mate preferences
- Is classified as a Group 1 Carcinogen The feminist movement credits birth control as a liberator of women, but the pill puts chains of chronic illness on millions of women.

Birth control is not a gift to women. It is a band aid solution to real issues women face that then enables women to keep working 50 hours a week. Pushing hormones on women that deplete key nutrients and functions in the body while dangling a carrot of reproductive freedom is NOT pro-women. Embrace your cycle. Lean into the phases of it. This creates HARMONY and peace in the body.

***The only safe form of birth control is Natural Family Planning. God created us to have babies!

*"Lo, children are an heritage of the
LORD: and the fruit of the womb is
his reward." (Psalm 127:3)*

HOW TO HAVE A HEALTHY PREGNANCY

"Hi Lori, After a long time trying, the Lord has blessed my husband and me with our first child. As you are a wise, God-fearing woman whose judgment I trust, I'm writing to you to ask if you have any advice for this pregnancy or any resources you would recommend I read. Lily"

Hi Lily,

For pregnancy, you simply need to eat as healthy as you can. I would recommend not using anything toxic to clean with or putting anything toxic on your hair or skin, not even on your finger nails such as nail polish. You want to give your baby the best chance of being healthy. We live in a toxic environment, so you must be diligent to stay as healthy as possible.

Eat organic food. Check out the Weston A. Price website. They have a lot of good articles. Eat food the way God created it to be eaten. Cut out sugar and processed food from your diet. Eat a lot of healthy fats (butter, extra virgin olive oil, ghee, avocado oil), protein (grass-fed beef, pastured eggs and chicken, wild-caught fish like sardines), and lots of vegetables. Eat probiotics such as kefir and sauerkraut.

Make sure you get outside as often as possible. Get sunshine on your skin. Exercise, like walking, is great for you. Sleep plenty at night. Rest when you're tired. Don't be fearful and anxious about what is going on in our country. Most generations that have ever lived have lived in turmoil. This isn't our home. Satan is the prince of the power of the air. Focus upon the good and lovely instead.

Be thankful for the many blessings the Lord has given to you.

Read books like "To Train Up a Child" and "Shepherding a Child's Heart" to prepare for raising godly offspring. Forget the "gentle parenting" movement of today that teaches parents to never say "no" to their children, never spank, and gives the child complete control. This is the recipe for raising a rebellious child! God's ways work for raising children. They try to convince us that Jesus was a gentle parent. God tells us He chastens and scourges every child whom He loves (Hebrews 12:6). Look up those two words.

I also encourage you to NEVER use a microwave to heat food up. It is radiation and destroys all of the nutrients in the food. I don't even heat my water in the microwave! I heat up everything in our little toaster oven or on the stovetop. The only thing we use our microwave for is to heat up our heating pads in the winter!

Be in God's Word daily. Become the wife and mother that God has called you to become! This will be the greatest blessing that you can give to your children. Be full of the joy of the Lord; for the joy of the Lord is your strength!

"Let the word of Christ dwell in you richly in all wisdom; teaching and admonishing one another in psalms and hymns and spiritual songs, singing with grace in your hearts to the Lord." (Colossians 3:16)

DOCTORS, DRUGS, AND DEMONS

My mom grew up in a church where doctors, drugs, and demons were synonymous. Her mom raised seven children without ever taking them to the doctor. Her home remedy for almost everything was warm water with fresh lemon and honey. Then my mom married a doctor. She developed ulcerative colitis when I was very young. She went to a doctor who put her on only "white food" and steroids, and told her that there was no cure. She grew sicker. She knew this wasn't going to work.

She went to "health farms" where they would fast her for several weeks on water only, then give her fresh juices from organic vegetables. After much trial and error, she was able to heal herself completely and even had a doctor do a colonoscopy to prove it to him. (Jordan Rubin from "The Maker's Diet" cured himself from the same disease.) If drugs, radiation, or surgery can't heal oneself, doctors will tell their patients that it's incurable.

I don't ever remember my mom giving me drugs for anything. We rarely went to the doctor. Therefore, my sisters and I grew up with a healthy fear of drugs. We all went to a large public school where drugs, alcohol, and fornication were rampant. (There was no homosexuality nor transgenderism back then and if there was, it certainly wasn't out in the open.) This was in the 1970s after the sexual revolution of "free love." (Satan sure likes to take what is evil like fornication and give it a good name like "free love." He's the master deceiver.)

Because all of us had a healthy fear of drugs, none of us were ever even tempted by them. Besides, I was relatively happy and didn't need anything to make me "happy" or deaden any pain in my life like many of my classmates did.

I read a post from a woman whose brother killed himself

with heroin. They weren't raised in a Christian home, but she became a strong believer in Jesus Christ later in life. She eventually led her brother to the Lord. He had to go to prison shortly afterwards and shared the Gospel with whomever would listen. He went to rehab facilities but could never stay sober for long. Oh, how he regretted ever taking the wicked stuff. It eventually took his life.

A beautiful woman I mentored was married to a man who became addicted to opiates due to a leg injury he sustained while being a firefighter. He went to a Christian rehab center, and then the two of them were reunited. Eventually, the fire department wanted to reinstate him, but she noticed something wasn't right about him. She asked him to test his urine and sure enough, he was back onto drugs and a destructive path.

Women, warn your children about the dangers of drugs. I rarely gave my children drugs growing up. Maybe a few Tylenol when they were in bad pain (Tylenol harms the liver so be careful!), but that's almost it. They grew up with a healthy fear of drugs. Yes, there is a time and place for drugs. They have saved many lives including mine, but they should be the last resort, not the first as many do these days. All drugs have side effects and need to be taken with care.

If you are raising your children in the Lord and to know who they are in Christ, they most likely won't turn to drugs. Their lives will have meaning. Many children are growing up in daycare, then being taught humanism in public schools. They're taught they came from apes, thus there's no meaning to their lives. This is such a lie! God formed them in your womb. He sent His Son to die for them to take the penalty of their sin so they could live eternally with Him. They need to hear this often!

"And thou shalt teach them diligently unto thy children, and shalt talk of them when thou sittest in thine house, and when thou walkest by the way, and when thou liest down, and when thou risest up." (Deuteronomy 6:7)

PROTECT YOUR HUSBAND'S AND SON'S SPERM

The NYT has an article entitled "What are Sperm Telling Us?" Here are some quotes from the article:

"Sperm counts have been dropping; infant boys are developing more genital abnormalities; more girls are experiencing early puberty; and adult women appear to be suffering declining egg quality and more miscarriages...Four years ago, a leading scholar of reproductive health, Shanna H. Swan, calculated that from 1973 to 2011, the sperm count of average men in Western countries had fallen by 59 percent. Inevitably, there were headlines about 'Spermageddon' and the risk that humans would disappear, but then we moved on to chase other shiny objects.

"Swan and other experts say the problem is a class of chemicals called endocrine disruptors, which mimic the body's hormones and thus fool our cells. This is a particular problem for fetuses as they sexually differentiate early in pregnancy. Endocrine disruptors can wreak reproductive havoc. These endocrine disruptors are everywhere: plastics, shampoos, cosmetics, cushions, pesticides, canned foods and A.T.M. receipts. They often aren't on labels and can be difficult to avoid."

Many of our modern conveniences are great but at what

cost? Are there things we can do about this? Yes! I know a couple who couldn't get pregnant due to the husband's low sperm count. He was put on a healthy, organic diet and months later, the wife was pregnant! I believe eating as much organic food as possible is very important since organic food isn't sprayed heavily with toxic chemicals like regular food is.

Even hand sanitizers are harmful to your health! There's also a professor who is concerned with the many children getting leukemia these days. "And this issue is becoming an increasingly worrying problem. Parents, for laudable reasons, are raising children in homes where antiseptic wipes, antibacterial soaps and disinfected floor washes are the norm. Dirt is banished for the good of the household." You don't need to be the perfect, spotless housekeeper who fears germs!

"Be careful for nothing; but in every thing by prayer and supplication with thanksgiving let your requests be made known unto God. And the peace of God, which passeth all understanding, shall keep your hearts and minds through Christ Jesus." (Philippians 4:6,7)

NON-TOXIC PRODUCTS FOR YOUR HOME AND BODY

Lotion/Moisturizer

- Dr. Bronner's Organic Hand/Body Lotion
- Think Sport Baby Body Lotion
- DIY Cream: 1/4 cup cocoa butter, 1/4 cup shea butter, 1/4 cup coconut oil, 1/4 cup sweet almond oil, 5-15 drops of pure essential oil

- Avalon Organics
- Skin Gel by Aloe Life (It's the only one that helps me dramatically with my dry skin!)
- Beef Tallow is great too!
- Weleda Skin Food is excellent for your face.

Baby Lotion/Moisturizer

- Babo
- Acure Unscented
- Weleda Baby Calendula
- Think Sport Baby Body Lotion
- Andalou Naturals
- Primally Pure

Bath Salts/Soaks

- Zum Tub Bath Salts
- DIY Detox Bath: 1 cup Epsom salt + 1 cup baking soda + Essential Oils
- DIY Salt & Vinegar Detox Bath: 1/4 cup Himalayan/Sea salt + 1/4 cup Epsom salt + 1/4 cup baking soda + 1/3 cup ACV + Essential Oils

Shampoo

- Acure (I use the Simply Smoothing Shampoo)
- Alaffia
- Attitude
- Dr. Bronner's
- Plaine Products
- Innersense Organics
- Rocky Mountain Soap Company

Dry Shampoo

- Acure
- Kaia Naturals
- Crunchi No Filter Translucent Finishing Powder
- DIY: 2 Tbsp organic cocoa powder + 2 Tbsp arrowroot powder OR organic cornstarch. It can be stored in a glass salt shaker

Hair Gel/Spray/Hair Dye/Personal Gel

- Innersense Organics
- Andalou Naturals
- Giovanni Hair Spritz (I love this!)
- No Nothing (This is a great Mousse for your hair with NO toxic chemical.)
- Herbatint Hair Dye is what I use to color my hair.
- Personal Gel Intimate Moisturizer by Aloe Life is a great lubricant for married couples.

Face Wash

- Crunchi Charcoal and/or Gentle Facial Bar
- Dulce de Donke bar soap
- Nourish Organics (all skin types)
- Dr. Bronner's
- Nourish Organic
- Zum Bar Goat's Milk Soap
- Norwex bath cloth – It's all I use to wash my face!

Baby Wash

- Earth Mama Angel Baby Organics
- Dr. Bronners Baby
- Wink Naturals
- Crunchi Gentle Cleansing Bar

Deodorant

- Crystal Body Deodorant Stick
- Piper Wai
- Dulce De Donke
- Primal Pit Paste
- Tom's Fragrance Free
- ThinkSport
- Primally Pure
- Essential Oils/CBD Oils
- Bluebird Botanicals
- Charlotte's Web
- Since I eat so healthy, I don't need deodorant!

Bug Repellent

- Badger
- Sky Organics
- Twinkle Apothecary (OKC)
- DIY – 8 oz dark glass spray bottle + 10 drops YL Purification + 5 drops Citronella + 5 drops Lavender + 5 drops Lemon + 5 drops Peppermint + 1/2 cup distilled water + 1/2 cup witch hazel (optional). Shake before each use.

Lip Balm/Chapstick

- Dr. Bronner's chapstick and/ or Magic Balm
- SkyOrganics
- Badger
- Hurraw Lip Balm
- Crunchi clear lip gloss
- Just Ingredients (I love this one!)

Hand Sanitizer

- Dr. Bronner's Lavender Spray
- Thieves Young Living

Sunscreen (all kid-friendly)

- Crunchi Sunlight (face)
- Thinksport/Thinkbaby
- Badger
- Earth Mama
- Babo Botanicals
- Goddess Garden
- All Good

Makeup

- Ilia is my favorite! I love their mascara, blush, and lipstick.
- Jane Iredale is another good one.

Laundry

- Molly's Suds Laundry Powder
- Buckaroo Organics Soapberry Suds
- DIY Laundry Powder – Castille soap, baking soda, and washing soda
- Wool Dryer Balls + Essential Oils
- Biokleen Laundry Liquid (This is the one I use! I used to make my own but I learned that Borax is questionable.)

Hand Soap

- Moon Valley Organics
- DIY: Combine 1/3 cup castille soap, 2/3 cup warm water, 1 tsp almond oil, 10-15 drops of

essential oils of your choice into a foam pump bottle

- Dr. Bronner's
- Crunchi Charcoal Body bar
- Rocky Mountain
- Dulce de Donke bar soap

Dishwashing Soap

- Chae Organics
- Better Life
- Seventh Generation Dish Liquid
- Dr. Bronner's Sal Suds (I love this!)

Dishwasher Detergent

- Ecover Automatic Dishwasher Tablets (This is what I use!)
- I read that a 1/2 teaspoon of dish soap works too!

Toothpaste

- Dr. Brite (Also has a teeth whitening pen)
- Dr. Bronner's
- Jason
- My Magic Mud
- Redmond Earth Paste
- Wellnesse Whitening Toothpaste (It's very expensive but works great! I use a tiny bit every morning so a tube lasts a long time for me.)

Cleaning Products

- Branch Basics
- Young Living Thieves Household Cleaner
- Dr. Bronner's Pure Castile Soap
- Force of Nature

- Norwex Enviro Cloth, Dusting Mitt, Window Cloth, Mop System
- Steam Mop
- I use the Norwex cleaning cloth and a bottle filled with 1/3 each of hydrogen peroxide, vinegar, and water with a squirt of dishwashing soap.

Cookware

- Cast Iron
- Glass Corningware
- Le Creuset Enameled Cast Iron & Stoneware
- Stainless Steel
- Stoneware
- X-trema

Apps to Verify Ingredients

- EWG
- Think Dirty

We must do all we can to protect the reproducing ability of our children. This impacts future generations; therefore, we must be as wise as serpents. Do your research. Eat as healthy as you can and use products that aren't harming your children's ability to have their own children.

*"What? know ye not that your body is the
temple of the Holy Ghost which is in you,
which ye have of God, and ye are not your
own? For ye are bought with a price: therefore,
glorify God in your body, and in your spirit,
which are God's." (1 Corinthians 6:19,20)*

LIVING A CANCER FREE LIFESTYLE

Cancer is a growing menace in our culture. I know too many women personally who are fighting this terrible disease and too many children and young adults who have died from this disease. We live in a toxic world. Yes, all of modern technology has made life a lot easier but it has come with great costs, namely, the cost to our health. We must be diligent in fighting these adverse side effects as much as possible but then leave the results in the Lord's hands. Even if we lived a perfectly toxic-free lifestyle, we can still die from cancer since, as I stated, we live in a toxic world. In this article, I'm going to share with you all of the ways I could think of trying to live a cancer free lifestyle.

I'll begin with the way I eat since Hippocrates (400 BC), known as the father of medicine stated, "Let food be thy medicine and medicine be thy food." He emphasized the importance of nutrition to prevent and cure disease. I believe the best thing I do daily to prevent cancer is to eat a big salad every day filled with romaine, arugula, and red leaf lettuce. Then I add radicchio, radishes, carrots, red peppers, avocado, tomatoes, sprouted pumpkin seeds, sardines (the best source of omega-3 fatty acids), and a couple of tablespoons of sauerkraut on it. I use my homemade salad dressing that is filled with healthy fats.

I eat almost only organic food and rarely eat out. I make big pots of vegetable soup with chicken broth filled with greens, potatoes, onions, yams, broccoli, and any other vegetables I want to add, and I have that for dinner many nights. We also eat organic, grass-fed beef, organic chicken, and wild caught fish. I make almost everything from scratch and have many of my family favorite dinner recipes which I shared with you at the beginning of this book. I make my own Einkorn sourdough bread and have made it so easy to make! Between my daughter, DIL, and sister, we have it down to a few easy steps.

I eat no sugar or junk food and try to eat food closest to the way God created for us to eat. I do have a healthy chocolate recipe that we all love, but I try to limit the sweets and fruits I eat however. Too much fructose isn't good either. Cancer feeds on sugar so limit all of it in your life as much as possible.

I make my own kefir which I have in the morning with a sprouted granola and blueberries, or I have pastured eggs on my sourdough bread. Recently, I have protein shakes with Paleo Pure Chocolate Protein, coconut milk, and frozen blueberries. It's gentle on my sensitive gut. Probiotics like kombucha, sauerkraut, and kefir are very important for a healthy gut. Good health begins and ends in the gut! Kefir is loaded with probiotics and has three times the amount of yogurt.

I don't drink coffee or alcohol. Caffeine is hard on the adrenals and stomach, and it's hard to remain completely sober while drinking alcohol. Caffeine and alcohol are drugs. I try to take as few drugs into my life as possible, and I don't want to be addicted to anything. (I am not saying that either of them are sinful in moderation.)

In our backyard, we have numerous types of fruit trees (fig, orange, lemon, apple, guava, tangerine, and peach). We have never sprayed our yard with any toxic ingredients. We've never sprayed for ants. I use a glass jar or any type of cylinder and roll that over the trail of ants. I leave the dead ants there, and their comrades come and pick them up and leave my home. I haven't had a problem with ants for over 15 years! Vinegar works well on weeds but picking them out from the roots works the best. I use organic fertilizers in my yard when and if needed. If I'm having a problem with pests or mold, I find natural ways to deal with them.

We use reverse osmosis to filter our water. Berkeys are great, too. Most tap water is filled with toxic chemicals, especially if you live in a big city. I try to sleep as much as possible at night in a dark, cool, and quiet room. I go to bed early. Sleep is very important for fighting cancer and lack of sleep increases your risk for some cancers. I don't use fluoride in my toothpaste. I believe fluoride is a toxic chemical. I only take drugs IF needed and use natural means for healing unless it's an emergency. Elderberry syrup is great for preventing and/or shortening colds and the flu. I believe vaccinations are damaging to health and cause cancer since they're filled with toxic ingredients and most probably aborted fetuses. I don't have mammograms. Smashing breasts and radiating them seems like it would cause cancer. Ultrasounds are far safer.

I take a walk almost every day of the year. Thankfully, we live in a climate that allows me to do this. Exercise is very important for good health. It's also good to be out in the fresh air and sunshine as much as possible. I sleep with a window open and have my windows open as much as possible during the day. The air in our homes is much more toxic than the air outside of our homes due to the carpets, furniture, and other things which I don't have, such as air fresheners, toxic cleaners, dryer sheets, and candles. Wood flooring and tile are much healthier than carpet since carpet is completely synthetic and harbors a lot of nasty things. We have mostly wood, and it's a breeze to keep clean. We never need to have a carpet company come out and clean our carpets. We have bought most of our furniture on Craig's List since it's outgassed by then. New furniture is full of toxic chemicals.

Most sunscreens are highly toxic. You must know that everything you put on your skin is absorbed into your body.

A friend of mine has used sunscreen on her face every single day and has never laid out in the sun but has had a TON of skin cancer on her face that she's needed extensive surgeries for. The best way to get vitamin D, which is a great cancer fighter, is from the sun. No, don't get burned or be out too long but sunshine is good for us! It causes everything to grow.

I clean with all non-toxic cleaners such as vinegar, hydrogen peroxide, Bar Keepers Friend, and a dash of non-toxic dishwashing soap. I use non-toxic dishwasher detergent, dish soap, body soap, and body lotion (For Christmas, my sister made me some body lotion and I love it!), make up, hair dye, and everything else. I stopped using nail polish immediately when I found out that a few hours after nail polish is applied, many of the harmful, toxic ingredients are in the person's blood stream. Blood tests have proven this to be so. Whenever I find out something is toxic, I stop doing it. I don't whiten my teeth, because the ingredients to do this are often toxic and it damages teeth.

What about radiation? We only use our microwave to heat up our heating pads. I don't use it to heat up food. Microwaves are dangerous. You can read a good article about this and many other great articles at the Weston A. Price website. I use only stainless steel and cast-iron skillets and pans. Never use the Teflon types. I don't put my cell phone to my ear. I use the speaker phone, and I have a radiation protector on my phone. It is ironic since I have had my head radiated to death with CT scans, MRIs, and CyberKnife. After CyberKnife, I drank a cup of organic green tea daily for months afterwards, since I have read that this is a good antidote to radiation. The CyberKnife killed my tear ducts so instead of regular eye drops, I use castor oil which works great.

I store all of my food in glass containers or mason jars.

The abundance of estrogen in plastics and in foods such as soy are wreaking havoc on people's health. This is why men's sperm count is tanking, and I believe why so many women struggle with infertility. We have too much estrogen in our water, food, and air. Make it a habit to read the ingredients of everything that you buy and stay away from anything with soy in it, has dyes in it, and chemicals. You want to eat food only.

I use very little makeup but what I do use is non-toxic. EWG.org is a good site to find out how toxic products are and be able to make wise choices. All drugs are toxic to the human body. Doctors are taught this in medical school, so drugs should always be used with discretion. I have had many things happen to me in my 65 years of life but have found many healthy, alternative ways to treat my body other than drugs.

If you can't afford all organic food, look up the dirty dozen and try to eat those organically. With Costco and Trader Joe's stocked full of organic foods, it's more cheaply available than ever before! Plant a garden and have some chickens if you are able. Look on EWG.org and find the best rated and cheapest products. Make your own laundry detergent. I did for years. There are many ways to afford living a cancer-free lifestyle if you put your mind to it.

Remember women, we do the best that we can, we don't worry about it, and we leave our lives in the hands of Almighty God. Our times are in His hands, and He gives out wisdom freely, so ask for it. I love what one woman wrote on my Instagram, "Clearly many of us are deceived into thinking this kind of lifestyle is unobtainable. Basically, I am taking baby steps to achieve these ideals. My Naturopath explained that real and lasting change is made slowly."

THE IMPORTANCE OF BREASTFEEDING YOUR BABIES

Jessica Martucci PhD and Anne Barnhill PhD wrote an article that was published for the American Academy of Pediatrics (AAP) explaining to health professionals why they need to stop describing breastfeeding as 'natural.' "Promoting breastfeeding as 'natural' may be ethically problematic, and, even more troublingly, it may bolster this belief that 'natural' approaches are presumptively healthier." They fear that because vaccinations aren't natural, then those who are into "natural" won't vaccinate their children, therefore, they want pediatricians to stop using the word "natural" when describing breastfeeding. Wait, it gets worse...

"These pockets of anti-vaccination sentiment tend to overlap with reliance on and interest in complementary and alternative medicine, skepticism of institutional authority (public schooling), and a strong commitment and interest in health knowledge, autonomy, and healthy living practices." They worry that those who are into "natural" will want to use alternative medicine, homeschool their children, and actually study for themselves ways to be healthy apart from medicine. Do you know how manipulative all of this is?

"This embrace of the 'natural' over the 'unnatural' appears in a variety of contemporary scientific and medical issues beyond vaccination, including rejection of genetically modified foods, a preference for organic over conventionally grown foods, and rejection of assisted reproductive technologies, as well as concerns over environmental toxins and water fluoridation." Where is freedom of choice? I try to stay away from GMOs since man has changed the way God made food. I eat organic food, because I don't want my food sprayed with toxic chemicals. I am concerned with the long-term side effects and moral implications of assisted reproductive technologies. I do my best to use non-toxic cleaners in my home and am against water fluoridation. This is all wrong in their eyes?

"Coupling nature with motherhood, however, can inadvertently support biologically deterministic arguments about the roles of men and women in the family (for example, that women should be the primary caretakers of children)." So modern medicine wants to manipulate language to get people on board with all they promote, even going so far as saying that women shouldn't be the primary caretakers of children? When I read this, I didn't know if I wanted to cry or be angry. This is heartbreaking! We must wake up to Satan's deceptions going on all around us, women, including in the medical profession and drug companies!

"Referencing the 'natural' in breastfeeding promotion, then, may inadvertently endorse a controversial set of values about family life and gender roles, which would be ethically inappropriate. Invoking the 'natural' is also imprecise because it lacks a clear definition." It's clear that they believe that having a father and mother in a home with children is "a controversial set of values about family life and gender roles" and this is "ethically inappropriate." I weep for this culture and the children. Please, women, protect your children from this insanity.

Doctors aren't gods. They don't know everything. This is why they are known for "practicing medicine." They are mostly taught drugs, radiation, and surgery in medical school. People depend upon them entirely too much for their health, in my opinion. It's natural to not inject your body with poisons. Vaccinations aren't natural. I don't think anyone would argue with this. They are created in laboratories by men. They have ingredients in them that aren't created for the human body, and there's a lot of speculation that aborted babies are used to study and make them.

Whether you vaccinate your children or not is entirely up to you and your husband. This topic shouldn't cause dissension among believers. We must allow others to come to their own conclusions and do what they feel is best without becoming contentious, angry, and mean. My conclusion is that vaccinations are not natural nor are they healthy, but breastfeeding my babies didn't cause me to come to this conclusion. Many women who breastfeed their babies vaccinate their children.

Breastfeeding IS natural! It's the food that God created for babies to live on the first year of their lives or so. It's perfect for them! Man cannot make anything close to as good as breast milk from a mother's breast. Mothers have been nursing their babies since Eve had her first baby! It's also natural for mothers to be home with their babies and children full time. Mothers instinctively know this no matter how hard they try to ignore it or say it isn't so. When my oldest daughter adopted a baby, she used an organic goat milk formula with all healthy ingredients.

I believe that mothers need to do in-depth research to have healthy families instead of always depending upon their doctors. Eat food the way God created it to be eaten! My dad was in the hospital or skilled care facility for a long time. A doctor told him he needs to drink four bottles of Ensure every day. Have you read the ingredients on the Ensure label? Some of the first ingredients listed are corn syrup, sugar, canola oil, and soy protein isolate. All of these are health destroying. They are not nourishing to the body. I would never drink these!

Whenever a doctor wants to give you a drug or do some type of test on you, research it! Research vaccinations, their ingredients, and side effects. Don't just trust doctors at their word. Many don't seem to understand the healing power of the body. They don't spend hardly any time studying nutrition or what makes a strong immune system. I have been able to heal many things that most people would take drugs for, but I do appreciate doctors for emergency situations and for diagnosis.

Doctors are taught in medical school that all drugs are toxic to the human body so be your own family's advocate, women. Ask the Lord for wisdom in your decisions. He will give it to you! Do your best and leave the outcome in the Lord's hands. If you want to live as naturally as possible, by all means do so regardless of what the medical profession wants you to believe!

"But we proved to be gentle among you,
as a nursing mother tenderly cares for her
own children." (1 Thessalonians 2:7)

WHY ORGANIC FOOD IS SO EXPENSIVE

My mom fed us organic foods since the time I was five years old. I mostly eat organic foods and fed it to my children when they were growing up. Yes, it's more expensive, but I don't want all of the toxic chemicals sprayed on foods that are conventionally grown.

I have been reading a book called "The Dirty Life: A Memoir of Farming, Food, and Love" by Kristin Kimball. Someone recommended it on one of the blogs I follow. It's not a Christian book. She's a feminist, and they lived together before marriage. She didn't want to take her husband's last name since she liked her last name and none of her married friends took their husband's last name. Her husband told her he would take her last name then because he didn't want their children to have hyphenated last names. (It shows the sorry state of today's feminized culture.)

After they married, she wanted a break from her husband and went to Maui for a job but while there, she figured this out: "It wasn't Mark or the farm or marriage I was trying to shake loose from but my own imperfect self, and even if I kept moving, she would dog me all the way around the world, forever." So, she went home.

They fought often about ways to do things on the farm even though he had farmed for many years, and she had only been a city, career woman up until they met. It clearly shows the trouble when there is no leader or head. She finally realized another great truth after her time in Maui: "Without me to struggle against, without the constant chaos of our first growing season, without the pressure of our impending wedding, he seemed to have found his own steady rhythm. I worked my way into it, looking for harmony this time, instead of conflict."

This book is about a couple who decided they wanted to farm without any chemicals (toxic or non-toxic) and grow almost all of their own food. They wanted to be able to sell the food year-round to families so it's quite an adventure that they took upon themselves. Their lives are difficult but rewarding. She learned to love it!

There are a few things that I want to point out from this book. The first one being God's curse to man after the Fall. "And unto Adam he said, Because thou hast hearkened unto the voice of thy wife, and hast eaten of the tree, of which I commanded thee, saying, Thou shalt not eat of it: cursed is the ground for thy sake; in sorrow shalt thou eat of it all the days of thy life; Thorns also and thistles shall it bring forth to thee; and thou shalt eat the herb of the field; In the sweat of thy face shalt thou eat bread, till thou return unto the ground; for out of it wast thou taken: for dust thou art, and unto dust shalt thou return" (Genesis 3:19).

Now, read what she wrote about organic farming: "My existence, from daybreak to dark, became focused on the assassination of weeds. Before that first year, I'd filed 'agriculture,' in the card catalog of my head, in the same general place as 'nature.' As in many things, I was so wrong. Farming, I discovered, is a great and ongoing war. The farmers are continually fighting to keep nature behind the hedgerow, and nature is continually fighting to overtake the field. Inside the ramparts are the sativas, the cultivated plants, soft and vulnerable, too highbred and civilized for fighting. Aligned with nature, there are the weeds, tough foot soldiers, evolved for battle."

Then she wrote why organic food is more expensive than conventionally grown food: "If you ever wonder why organic vegetables cost more, blame the weeds. The work on a conventional farm that can be done with one pass of the sprayer must, on an organic farm, be done continually, from germination to harvest, by physically disrupting the weeds." It's a lot easier to spray crops with a bunch of toxic chemicals that kill weeds than it is to deal with the weeds without the chemicals which this couple and many other organic farmers do. Organic farmers take on God's curse, and conventional farmers have learned how to avoid it with great cost to the health of many.

This couple's cows grazed on clover and grass in the warmer weather and on hay (that they had made) during the cold months instead of on GMO corn like conventional cows are fed today. All of their animals ate the foods they were created to eat, thus the eggs and meat they provided were nutritious and built up one's health instead of tearing it down.

The toxic chemicals that conventional farmers use isn't only killing the weeds. They are killing the worms which make the soil rich and full of nutrients, and the crops soak up the toxic chemicals that people eat. The chemicals are killing our bees which are essential, and they are polluting our environment. Then we wonder why cancer rates are so high today.

I shop at a locally owned health food store. All of their produce is organic and marked with labels that tell where and how far away the food was produced so we are getting food that isn't sprayed with chemicals and is freshly picked. Along with eating organic foods, I have learned to make Einkorn Sourdough bread, kefir, fermented vegetables, and chicken broth. None of these things are very expensive, but it's worth it to do what I can for good health then leave the rest in the Lord's hands. Man cannot improve upon food the way God created it to be eaten.

"The average cost of cancer is $150,000 per treatment. The standard American diet and toxin consumption is known to cause cancer. Do not tell me living a healthier lifestyle is expensive; pay now or pay later." (Tania the Herbalist on Instagram)

THE POWER OF FEVERS FOR GOOD

Many people today literally live in fear of having a fever. My mom raised us to not fear them at all but understood that it was the body's way to rid itself of viruses and disease. I raised my children the same way. I would give them a lot of warm water with fresh lemon juice and organic, raw honey just like my grandmother did with her seven children. (Nowadays, I have also added elderberry syrup for any colds or flu, and it's so easy to make!)

I used Dr. Mendelsohn's book "How to Raise a Healthy Child in Spite of Your Doctor" all the time when I was raising children. He had a medical partner that was older than him who attended medical school when they were still taught the amazing healing powers of the human body. Dr. Mendelsohn learned a lot from him and throughout his 30 years of being a pediatrician, he found that many times the body just needs rest and nourishment to fight most diseases. Here is an excerpt from his book about fevers since this seems to frighten many mothers today:

"If your child contracts an infection, the fever that accompanies it is a blessing, not a curse. It occurs because of the spontaneous release of pyrogens that cause the body temperature to rise. This is a natural defense mechanism that our bodies employ to fight disease. The presence of fever tells you that the repair mechanisms of the body have gone into high gear.

"The process works like this: When an infection develops, your child's body responds by manufacturing additional white blood cells, called leukocytes. They destroy bacteria and viruses and remove damaged tissue and irritating materials from the body. The activity of the white cells is also increased, and they move more rapidly to the site of the infection. This part of the process, called leucotaxis, is stimulated by the release of the pyrogens that raise body temperature. Hence the fever. A rising body temperature simply indicated that the process of healing is speeding up. It is something to rejoice over, not to fear.

"But that isn't all that's happening. Iron, which many germs need in order to thrive, is being removed from the blood and stored in the liver. This reduces the rate at which the bacteria multiply. The action of interferon, a disease-fighting substance produced naturally in the body, also becomes more effective.

"Artificially induced fevers have been used in laboratory experiments with animals to demonstrate this process. Elevated temperatures decrease the death rate among animals infected with disease, but if their body temperatures are lowered, more of them die. Artificially induced temperatures have actually been used for many years to treat diseases in humans that do not normally produce fevers themselves.

"If your children have a fever resulting from infection, resist the temptation to use drugs or sponging to bring it down. Let the fever run its course. If parental sympathy impels you to do something to relieve your child's discomfort, sponge him off with tepid water or give him one tablet of acetaminophen of the strength recommended for his age. Do nothing beyond that unless the fever persists for more than three days, or other symptoms develop, or your child looks and acts really sick. In that event, see your doctor.

"I want to emphasize that, while reducing his fever may make your child more comfortable, you may interfere with the natural healing process if you do it. My only reason for discussing methods of temperature reduction is the probability that some parents won't be able to resist doing it. If you are going to do it, sponging is preferable to drugs because of the risks associated with aspirin and acetaminophen. Despite the frequency of their use, these are far from innocuous drugs.

"Your child's cold, influenza, or any other infection will not produce a fever that exceeds 106 degrees, and below that level the fever will not cause any lasting harm. Because your child's bodily defenses won't allow infections to produce fevers of 106 degrees, you need not live in fear of mental or physical damage when his temperature begins to rise. I doubt that many pediatricians, including those who have practiced for decades, have seen more than one or two cases of fever above 106 degrees during their entire careers. Those that did see were the result of causes other than infection, such as poisoning or heatstroke.

"I have treated tens of thousands of children, and I've seen only one case of fever higher than 106. That's not surprising, because it is estimated that 95 percent of childhood fevers don't even reach 105.

"It is estimated that only 4 percent of children with high fever experience fever-related convulsions. There is no evidence that those who do have them suffer any serious aftereffects as a result. One study of 1,706 children who had suffered febrile convulsions failed to disclose a single death or motor defect. There is also no convincing evidence that febrile seizures in childhood increase susceptibility to epilepsy later in life."

DR. MENDELSOHN'S QUICK REFERENCE GUIDE TO FEVER

- If your child is less than two months of age and his temperature exceeds 100 degrees, call your doctor.

- For older children it is unnecessary to call the doctor unless the fever fails to abate within three days or is accompanied by other major symptoms.

- Call your doctor, regardless of temperature level, if the child is experiencing difficulty in breathing, vomiting repeatedly, or strange movements.

- If your child experiences chills along with his fever, don't try to counteract by piling on more blankets. Chills are the body's way of adjusting to higher temperatures.

- Encourage your feverish child to rest, but don't make too big a production of it.
- If you have reason to believe that the fever is the result of a cause other than infection, such as heat stroke or poisoning, take your child to a hospital emergency room at once.
- Ignore the old wives' tale "Feed a cold and starve a fever." Nourishment is an important part of recovery from any illness.
- Make sure they are getting plenty of fluids.

"I will praise thee; for I am fearfully and wonderfully made: marvelous are thy works; and that my soul knoweth right well." (Psalm 139:14)

WORKING HARD IN MY KITCHEN

As keepers at home, one of our main ministries to our family and others is learning to cook. During the 60s and the feminist movement when women left their homes to go out and pursue careers, fast food restaurants and packaged foods became popular; anything to make the working mothers' lives easier. Now, we have several generations of women who don't cook at all or don't like to cook, and our nation's health is suffering as a result. It's important to learn to enjoy working hard in your kitchen!

My sister didn't like to cook at all when she was raising her children. She did it a bit to keep her family fed, but it certainly wasn't something she enjoyed. Then she got malignant melanoma and radically changed her diet. Now, she loves cooking nourishing food in her kitchen, and we all love eating at her house. It was all simply a change of attitude, she told me. She puts on praise music and prays over the people she is preparing food for since she has learned to love it. (She made us the most wonderful Thanksgiving dinner one year!)

When our out-of-town family comes to stay with me, I prepare for their arrival. I make my Organic Einkorn Bread every day for a week to store up for them. My son-in-law, who can't have gluten, LOVES it so I want to make sure that I have plenty for him. (It really is easy to make, women. It looks complicated but once you start going, it doesn't take much time at all, and it's so much healthier than anything you can get in the store.) It is a labor of love, but I love making healthy and great tasting food for my family.

For breakfast, I have my homemade kefir that is so easy to make and full of healthy probiotics, calcium, and protein. In fact, Dr. Marshall, who I listened to for years, and Dr. Axe believe it is one of the most probiotic-rich foods on the planet! I much prefer making it than buying it since the homemade stuff is much less expensive and so rich and creamy like yogurt. I add a bit of stevia and frozen or fresh berries with it. On other mornings, I will have some of my Einkorn bread slathered with raw, grass-fed butter, topped with pastured eggs. I love my breakfasts!

About every four days or so, I make a large salad that we eat every night. On top of it, we put roasted chicken, avocado, a tablespoon of fermented vegetables (great for gut health which is imperative for good health), steamed beets (great for your blood), and anything else we feel like putting on it, then top it off with my homemade salad dressing that is loaded with healthy fats. I know that I have felt a lot better since I've added a lot of healthy fats and proteins to my diet. My sister taught me a delicious way to eat sardines since they are one of the healthiest fish you can eat and are the highest source of omega-3 fatty acids on the planet!

For dinner, I have a large mug full of my soup made with chicken broth and lots of vegetables. (I cooked a lot of heartier meals for my children when they lived with us. I still make pizza and other more filling food for my husband, however. He does have a big salad almost every night!)

My very favorite dessert in the entire world is my healthy chocolate that is made with coconut oil, walnuts, and raw cacao so it actually builds up our body instead of tearing it down. I like it best with raw, organic honey.

I also research and learn ways to keep my family healthy without drugs. I believe building up the immune system and using natural means of healing gives better results without the side effects of drugs. Our bodies were created to be able to fight most illnesses if nourished on good food. I make elderberry syrup for colds and flu and so far, it's worked amazingly. I also have other things I use in my arsenal to fight colds, flu, and all types of infections.

Teach your daughters to help you in the kitchen. From a young age, teach them to clean off their plate and put it in the dishwasher. As they grow older, you can have them right by your side helping you cook and clean your kitchen. Their future husband and children will appreciate the time and effort that you put into teaching them to enjoy working hard in their kitchen.

Yesterday, I made a big salad and salad dressing, roasted a chicken and made chicken broth, made a sardine salad, and two loaves of bread. Yes, I worked hard in my kitchen and I didn't mind one bit!

"And whatsoever ye do, do it heartily, as to the Lord, and not unto men; Knowing that of the Lord ye shall receive the reward of the inheritance: for ye serve the Lord Christ." (Colossians 3:23, 24)

WHAT ABOUT ALCOHOL?

This was written by Natural Nurse Momma on Twitter. She is a wealth of information!

A study out of Canada from 2022 showed that NO amount of alcohol is safe. "Even a single dose of alcohol-ethanol-can PERMANENTLY alter synapses and mitochondrial movement in the brain's neurons." Alcohol increases the risk of SEVEN different types of cancer. Alcohol shuts down methylation, is a DISINFECTANT hurting your gut, it clogs your liver, depletes your nutrients, and decreases white matter in your brain.

"Studies demonstrate that women who consume about 1 drink per day have a 5 to 9 percent higher chance of developing breast cancer than women who do not drink at all. That risk increases for every additional drink they have per day."

Chronic alcohol use increases blood pressure, is a leading cause of heart disease, it causes fibrosis and fatty deposits in the liver (hello hormonal problems). Another factor is alcohol irritates the gut lining and causes inflammation. Less nutrients are absorbed which further contributes to body dysfunction. It raises your cortisol, decreases REM sleep, and accelerates aging.

The effects of chronic alcohol use are widespread and numerous. Alcohol causes blood sugar dysregulation and is a contributing factor to the massive epidemic of insulin resistance in our country. This country normalizes having a drink every day, binge drinking is "a part of being a young adult." It doesn't have to be, and it shouldn't.

Hollywood glorifies it. From Bad Moms to every other movie and TV show... it makes it seem normal to "need a drink" ... but is Hollywood seeing the medical bills? Hospitals have seen a 30-50 percent increase in alcoholism, the biggest uptick is women under 40. Alcohol is a factor in 30 percent of car accidents in this country. "Thirty-two people in the United States are killed every day in crashes involving an alcohol-impaired driver—this is one death every 45 minutes."

Alcohol isolates you. Alcohol depletes you. Alcohol changes you. Alcohol numbs you until it doesn't anymore. Then you are left depleted and not able to think clearly, less able to handle stress, and more likely "need" another drink.

If you do have a drink, think about quality. Between contaminants in alcohol to glyphosate on the grapes used to make wine, think about quality. As well, think about NAC, BodyBio. PC to stabilize the cell membrane, thiamine, dandelion root tea, Vitamin C, zinc, and a good B complex. Also consider a binder after drinking to help with the histamine response (I like Takesumi Supreme).

"Wine is a mocker, strong drink is raging: and whosoever is deceived thereby is not wise." (Proverbs 20:1)

DANGERS OF NAIL POLISH AND NAIL POLISH REMOVER

My mom was raised during and right after the Great Depression. Foods weren't sprayed with toxic chemicals back then, and the meat and dairy were from animals that ate what God created them to eat and lived how God created them to live (not crammed into small places). She grew up with four sisters and two brothers, and my mom was the one who was most health conscious. She mostly ate organic food and was basically healthy all of her life until she was 80 years old.

When she turned 80, she was diagnosed with multiple myeloma. It is a cancer that forms in a type of white blood cell called a plasma cell. Plasma cells help you fight infections by making antibodies that recognize and attack germs. Multiple myeloma causes cancer cells to accumulate in the bone marrow, where they crowd out healthy blood cells.

We've been trying to figure out how she got cancer since she lived to prevent it. Yes, we know there are no guarantees in life but after reading and studying about the dangers of nail polish and nail polish remover, we think we figured it out. She had her fingers and toenails done for probably 30 years on a consistent basis. From everything I have read about it, it is something we should all avoid due to how toxic and dangerous it is. Having pretty nails isn't worth getting cancer, and cancer is usually in one's body many years before it is diagnosed.

"One of the most insidious routes of solvent exposure and toxicity is through fingernail polish and fingernail polish remover. Young girls are especially susceptible to the toxic and xeno hormonal effects of solvents, and yet they are the ones most likely to have a dozen different shades of fingernail polish in their bedroom. In addition, solvents can damage a developing fetus in very small amounts and should be studiously avoided in any amount by pregnant women. It should be required by law (and is in some states) that labels on nail polish contain warnings to pregnant women, and that beauty salons have warning signs in areas where nail polish is applied and removed," wrote Dr. John R. Lee.

"Then they tested participants' urine for levels of diphenyl phosphate, or DPHP, a chemical created when the body metabolizes TPP. They compared the results to urine samples participants had submitted before the experiment and found that while DPHP levels didn't change very much in the participants who used gloves and fake nails, levels of DPHP increased sharply in the women who had received nail polish directly on their nails."

"'Big job' employees are veterans, experts at sculpting false nails out of acrylic dust. It is the most lucrative salon job, yet many young manicurists avoid it because of the specter of serious health issues, including miscarriage and cancer, associated with inhaling fumes and clouds of plastic particles." (Anna Almendrala from Huffington Post)

Here is a list of all of the chemicals in nail polish and nail polish remover.

"Nail polish is likely the most toxic cosmetic there is. Polish includes poisonous substances such as formaldehyde, phthalates, acetone, toluene, and benzophenones. Phthalates, solvents for colors, are toxic to the nervous system; acetone and toluene, which keep the color in liquid form, evaporate quickly and fill the air with noxious fumes, putting your respiratory system at risk. The other substance we fingered, benzophenones, may cause cancer."

There are some better choices of nail polish but even with them, the author of this article wrote, "I've shared our top picks below, but it is important to note that even these safer options still have some chemicals in them and I wouldn't use them all the time." I have decided to never use nail polish again.

We all know how toxic it is just by how it smells. Whenever

I did my nails, Ken would ask me to go to another room because of the toxic smell. It doesn't take research to figure this out but too many of us care more about our nails being pretty rather than the long-term consequences of it. All those years my mom was getting her nails done, she never wore anything over her mouth and nose to protect her from the fumes. Even then, the toxic chemicals entered her blood stream through her nail bed. Do most men even care about or notice women's painted fingernails and toenails??? It's not worth the risk, women.

"What? know ye not that your body is the temple of the Holy Ghost which is in you, which ye have of God, and ye are not your own? For ye are bought with a price: therefore glorify God in your body, and in your spirit, which are God's." (1 Corinthians 6:20)

CANCER RISING AMONG CHILDREN

Did you know that cancer is the number two killer among children ages five to fourteen years old according to the CDC? Just recently, I heard of a mother who was pregnant with her third baby and they saw a mass in the baby's abdomen, so they took the baby when the mother was only eight months along. The mass was a cancerous tumor that had spread throughout the baby's body. The baby died shortly afterwards. I grieve for this poor family. This ought not be. Children in the womb being diagnosed with cancer?

My parents once told me that they never heard of anyone having cancer back when they were young but now, we all know someone who has had it or died from it. It's rampant! It's killing our children, so something must be done. No, it's not finding more treatments for it which all have deadly side effects (like chemo). It's living to the best of our ability to prevent it!

Dr. Mendelsohn, a pediatrician for 30 years and the author of "How to Raise a Healthy Child in Spite of Your Doctor," wrote in 1984, "There is a growing suspicion that immunization against relatively harmless childhood diseases may be responsible for the dramatic increase in autoimmune diseases since mass inoculations were introduced. These are fearful diseases such as cancer, leukemia, rheumatoid arthritis, multiple sclerosis, Lou Gehrig's disease, lupus erythematosus, and the Guillain-Barre syndrome...Have we traded mumps and measles for cancer and leukemia?"

It has been commonly stated that people live much longer now due to our advanced medical care and vaccinations. Is this true? Our first president, George Washington, lived until he was 67 years old and died in 1799, Thomas Jefferson until 83 and died in 1826, John Adams until 90 and died in 1826, James Monroe until 73, and James Madison until 85. (You can see that the ages of the deaths of our presidents haven't changed much even with the advancements in medical care and vaccinations.) Every single drug and vaccination has many side effects. Type 2 Diabetes and the cost to treat it just may bankrupt our country, and it is completely reversible with diet. (More than 100 million Americans have diabetes or prediabetes). Yet, Hippocrates, the father of modern medicine, said, "Let food be your medicine and medicine be your food!"

I have been reading a book written by Dr. John R. Lee and he wrote a lot about our toxic environment and how damaging it is to our health. He often mentioned the xenoestrogens that are in our food and environment that raise potent estrogen levels which cause havoc on our health. "Anyone who eats non-organic meat and dairy products is eating these compounds and they are all potent estrogens. They can accumulate in our fatty tissues (breast, brain, and liver) and cause estrogen dominance, with all of its attendant symptoms." They are found in detergents (including dishwashing detergents), cosmetics and other toiletries, perfumes, plastics, carpeting, computers, herbicides, spermicides, and even condoms. (I quit using spermicide in my diaphragm when I was 23 years old and read on the label that it could cause cancer!) Nail polish and remover are "one of the most insidious routes of solvent exposure and toxicity." He encourages people to shop 'green' and eat organic foods, if they want to stay healthy.

God created our food perfect for us and if we want to avoid cancer, we need to get back to His perfect ways. My sister taught me to make sourdough Einkorn bread, and it's how our ancestors used to make bread. It is the superior ancient grain that hasn't been hybridized, made without yeast (which is bad for you if you have gut problems), and is easily digestible. Yes, it takes a lot more time to make but working hard in the kitchen is a good thing. (The fermentation process predigests the gluten so even those who are gluten sensitive can eat this bread with no problems.) She has also taught me how to make fermented vegetables which are very good for your gut. (Health begins and ends in the gut!) She taught me how to make sardine salad (like tuna salad but much better) that tastes amazing! (Sardines are full of omega 3s and other healthy things, anti-inflammatory, and they aren't contaminated like the larger fish.)

On my Instagram, I have been using it to teach women how to eat healthy, since it's so important. We all need to eat, so why not fix food that is nutritious and great tasting for our family! Let food be our medicine. Work on building a strong immune system since this is what fights off disease. We all have cancer cells in our body but a healthy body can fight them off. Stop eating sugar, seed oils, packaged food, and all of the other health destroying foods and get busy in the kitchen making food that will help your family stay healthier. We do what we can and leave the rest in the Lord's hands.

LIVING A LONG AND HEALTHY LIFE

Shirali Mislimov of Azerbaidzhan, U.S.S.R allegedly lived to be 168 years old and died in 1973. In researching his life, I found some interesting things. Now, I'm not interested in living that long but I do try to live as healthy as I can while I live. Yes, there are some things that have happened to me beyond what I could prevent like head and neck trauma that most likely caused my brain tumor and caused me to need a neck fusion. But we can learn from people who live to ripe old ages such as this man, and he was even working hard on the day he died!

What were some of his secrets to longevity and health?

He worked hard. "He had worked all day every day until age 165, he said, grazing sheep, riding horseback, chopping wood, and tending the fruit garden he had begun over a century earlier." God created us to work and not sit all day like most of us do. All generations before us had to work hard to survive, and there are some jobs that demand a lot of hard work. Hard work never killed anyone. It's good for us! "The soul of the sluggard craves and gets nothing, while the soul of the diligent is richly supplied" (Proverbs 13:4).

If you are home full time, make sure you get outside as often as possible with your children. They need a lot of movement and fresh air. Most children today sit in front of some type of screen all day, and this is why our nation is becoming more and more unhealthy. Take long walks or hikes. Find hobbies that you enjoy doing outside. Get away to somewhere quiet and unpolluted once in a while like the ocean or mountains. It's good for health and the soul. We live in a noisy and polluted world. I remember hearing that noise pollution is the hardest on the body! Have quiet times without distractions. I love peace and quiet.

He lived an "unhurried pace of life." We live under way too much stress today. Turn off the news! I can only handle a little bit of it and then I turn it off since there's nothing I can do about it except to pray anyway. Learn to eat slowly and enjoy your food. Learn to appreciate boredom, if you get to have it. Use this time to read another chapter in the Bible, read an inspirational book, or cook something good for dinner.

He lived a moderate life like we are instructed to do. "And every man that striveth for mastery is temperate in all things" (1 Corinthians 9:25). "Mislimov often told scientists who came to interview him that he had lived as long as he had largely by not smoking, drinking, napping during the day, or in any way losing control of his appetites." If we are believers in Christ Jesus, we are filled with the Spirit and one of the fruits of the Spirit is self-control. Therefore, we can be controlled with all of our appetites and live moderate lives! Believe it to be so and discipline your body by making it your slave instead of allowing it to control you.

He "did not smoke or drink, but ate fruits, vegetables, wholemeal bread, chicken broth, low-fat cheese and yogurt." He ate a simple diet and was most likely content on it, unlike most of us. "The longevity of Muslimov was linked to a diet of dairy and yogurt in particular." Yogurt is a fermented food and full of probiotics. Many studies have proven the effectiveness of probiotics for good gut health. Drugs, processed foods, and sugar destroy probiotics so it's best to give them up!

Did you notice he didn't eat any sugar or desserts? I just read an article this past week that if you want a good sex life, give up sugar! Your health will greatly improve just by giving this up. It may even help those of you who struggle with infertility. Also, one woman is reading a book about moods and depression in the chat room and has found that caffeine and alcohol are serotonin killers and a huge cause of depression and mood swings. Alcohol is another thing that is good to give up. because most grapes are the most sprayed crop on the planet so one glass of wine is a cocktail full of toxic chemicals.

It doesn't sound like there were any vaccinations or drugs either. If the people in this area were loading up on all of these foods to create good gut health, it makes sense. "Infectious diseases are rare in Azerbaidzhan, and heart ailments are all but unknown." They most likely didn't run to the doctor for every little cough, flu, rash, and fever but allowed their bodies to heal themselves with fresh air, good food, and rest.

Sounds like great recommendations to live a long and healthy life if the Lord so blesses you!

"Beloved, I wish above all things that thou mayest prosper and be in health, even as thy soul prospereth" (3 John 1:2).

PREVENTING DEPRESSION IN YOUNG PEOPLE

Young people seem to be experiencing depression more now than ever before. I found an article explaining eight reasons why this is the case. Most of these reasons are due to our prosperous, industrialized and fast-moving society. We think technology and our comfortable lifestyles are good, but they have come at a huge price to our health and the health of our children.

One of the main reasons is that mothers are no longer home raising their own children. Daycare and public schools are doing this. Babies need to have their mothers home full time for them to bond to their mothers. These babies grow up to be far more emotionally stable and secure than those who didn't have mothers at home full time. This provides the security and stability that children need. Read "The Way Home" by Mary Pride. She has extensive research on this subject.

The first reason listed is a lack of play. Do you see children playing in your streets and parks anymore? When I was growing up, we were playing outside most of the time, when the weather allowed. We didn't have a lot of toys so we used our imaginations to play. It is SO imperative that your children are outside playing as much as possible using their large muscles to run, jump, climb, etc. besides the benefits of being in the sunshine and fresh air.

C-Sections are also another factor. Way too many c-sections are given today. Yes, there are times when they must be given, but if at all possible, don't have a c-section. Natural births are, by far, the healthiest for baby and mother. Recovering from a natural birth is much quicker for the mother and the least number of drugs you can put into your body, the better since ALL drugs are toxic to the human body.

Sugar. The more we find out about sugar, the more we find that most diseases are from eating sugar. Sugar robs your body of important nutrients, allows cancer to proliferate, and beats down your immune system. Do all you can to prevent your children from eating sugar and seed oils. There are so many alternative healthy foods. I properly prepare all types of nuts and sunflower seeds for snacks. Popcorn popped in coconut oil and fruit are all great snacks for your children. Train your children to snack on nutritious food, instead of junk food which results in junk health.

Antibiotics are another reason for so much depression in children. My boys never had antibiotics growing up. My daughters received a little bit for ear infections until I learned that ear infections clear up just as quickly with antibiotics as they do without, yet those ear infections cured without antibiotics don't come back. I found this to be true. Dr. Marshall believes all infections can be cured without drugs, except a tooth infection which needs to be fixed. I have cured bladder infections, sinus infections, breast infections, and ear infections all without drugs. Drugs should only be used in emergency situations.

Television is robbing our children of mental health also. It prevents them from playing, using their imaginations, and relating with others. It is damaging to their developing brains and eyes. Some education experts believe that a child should not watch television until they are five or six years old. Then it should only be for an hour a day. It is addicting. Little children will be happily playing until they get in front of a television. Then they don't move at all!

How many times have I written about the devastation of divorce on children? Many times. God hates divorce and commands us to be covenant keepers for many reasons, and one of those reasons is for the sake of the children. I have seen the devastation divorce is upon even grown children. The value of a husband and wife staying united as one for all of their days can never be overestimated. Stay married, even if it isn't easy, because in the long run, it will be better for many.

Toxins are another cause of depression. I have already written a lot about the need for eating organic food, cleaning with non-toxic cleaners, and having your windows open as much as possible. We weren't created to live in a toxic environment, yet we all live in one. Do what you can to rid your family's life of toxins and then leave the rest in the Lord's hands.

Stress is the final cause of depression. Children are so stressed out today, especially if they are in the public schools with all of the competition and bullying. I never studied for the SAT. I didn't even have much homework in high school. We were allowed to be children and have a lot of play time. Most of today's children don't have this privilege. Do what you can to give your children a stress-free lifestyle.

Finally, the very most important thing this article left out is to teach the Gospel to your children early and often so they know clearly who they are in Christ and their precious value to the kingdom of God.

"May the God of hope fill you with all joy and peace in believing, so that by the power of the Holy Spirit you may abound in hope" (Romans 15:13).

WHAT IS A HEALTHY WEIGHT AND DIET

There is a lot of conflicting information out there about what is a healthy weight and diet. It seems to change from month to month according to the "last study." Here is a woman's response to this dilemma from a comment on another blog which is no longer active. I think you all will enjoy it!

There is much confusing information out there, no doubt. I used to be confused and not sure who to believe and what to follow. Not so much anymore. I've learned to listen to my body and not all the noise and information out there. I follow a few simple rules and discard the rest: eat real, traditional foods as prepared and consumed by our ancestors, eat a lot of healthy fats (animal foods are key) from healthy sources, and avoid sugar and anything processed. Get lots of sun, go barefoot, go to bed earlier (still working on that one), reduce stress, avoid as much as possible chemicals and toxins in my home and work environments, and spend more time outside, exercise when I feel like it, and laugh and have fun. I don't worry about the rest."

Being healthy, by the way, is the main thing to focus on. Too many people focus on losing weight. But losing weight should be a side-effect of getting healthy. When you get healthy from eliminating chemicals, toxins, processed foods, etc. and detoxing, you will naturally lose the weight and arrive at what's healthy for your own body, and that's different for different folks.

I don't worry about eating too much fat. I eat until I am satisfied. I don't worry about exercising myself to death to "keep in shape." I haven't had a weight problem ever in my life, but I have had trouble gaining weight, so when I started concentrating on eating real, whole foods as nature intended, I started to gain weight appropriately and now am at the most normal weight I've ever been in my life. These myths mouthed over and over again by medical experts are just nonsense anyway, and I know it's nonsense because my whole life (over six decades) I've observed people doing what they are told by mainstream health authorities and not getting well and not losing weight.

So, I have stopped consulting experts and just listen to my own intuition and common-sense knowledge. If you are constantly changing what you do because someone told you to do it but not thinking about why you are doing it or waiting to observe whether it works, then I can see why there is confusion. Stop listening to experts and do your own research. Ultimately, you have to do what works for you.

If you don't have digestive issues, you are most fortunate. Most people in the modern world do either from diet or poor lifestyle choices or both. These don't always appear as what you would think of as digestive issues. Sometimes they are masked in some other way. If you have chronic health issues, no matter who you are, you definitely have some digestive issues as all health begins in the gut. Holistic medicine recognizes that everything is connected – nothing is compartmentalized. If you aren't digesting your food properly, the eventual result is chronic health problems. I would have never connected my health issues to digestive problems, as my most noticeable symptoms weren't really digestive-related, or so I thought. Something to think about.

*"For everything created by God is good,
and nothing is to be rejected if it is received
with gratitude" (1 Timothy 4:4).*

DO YOU CATER TO YOUR TASTE BUDS?

Do you cater to your taste buds? Do you only eat something because it tastes good without having any idea what is in it and what it does to your health? I want to encourage you to STOP! Everything you put into your mouth affects your health. It doesn't just go in one end and out the other.

Food is meant to nourish our bodies. Sure, a treat once in a while is okay but why not make that treat something that does not have these ingredients in them like the Nestle Hot Cocoa Mix:

> Sugar, Corn Syrup Solids, Dairy Product Solids, Vegetable Oil({Partially hydrogenated coconut or palm kernel and hydrogenated soybean), Cocoa Processed with Alkali, and less than 2% salt, Cellulose Gum, Sodium Caseinate, Dipotassium Phosphate, Sodium Aluminosilicate, Mono- and Diglycerides, Guar Gum, Artificial Flavor, Sucralose.

There is not one healthy, nourishing item in this list. Sugar is very detrimental to your health, and it is the first several ingredients. Hydrogenated oils are not even fit for human consumption and then there are chemicals that should not be ingested into the human body.

Instead, fix some organic milk (raw milk if you can find it) or coconut milk with organic cocoa powder, a little bit of stevia or raw honey, and a pinch of salt. This will be far healthier for you; real food and nutritious. If you want a power bar, you can buy ones at the health food store with healthy ingredients or make your own from scratch. Cookies are easy to make with REAL ingredients; ingredients you can pronounce and food that hasn't been overly processed in any way, as I have given to you in my dessert recipes.

We shouldn't depend upon our health care system to keep us healthy. Yes, they are wonderful to have in emergency situations, but we need to be responsible for what is going into our bodies. Therefore, stop catering to your taste buds and cater to your body instead. Nourish it with food that will create good health and a strong body. Work on building a strong immune system and then go out and be salt and light to a dark and decaying world!

"Whether therefore ye eat, or drink, or whatsoever ye do, do all to the glory of God" (1 Corinthians 10:31).

MY GRANDMA REFUSED TO VACCINATE HER CHILDREN

Years ago, Good Morning America reported that there is a measles outbreak. They said 95 percent of those getting measles were not vaccinated. (Apparently, it wasn't that big of a deal since it wasn't on the news for long. Another example of how the media greatly exaggerates things.) I tried finding the side effects of measles versus the side effects of the measles vaccination, and it is difficult to find the side effects of the vaccination. Almost all of the websites are written by the drug companies, the government or by doctors, all who have a vested interest in the vaccinations. I have read that if you want to find the true side effects of vaccinations, you must read the insert that comes in the box of the vaccination, which most parents never see. Most would think twice if they knew the true, long-term side effects of all those vaccinations they are putting into their children. Besides, they want to give children 49 vaccinations before they are 6 years old!

This is what the CDC said are the symptoms of measles:

"A typical case of measles begins with mild to moderate fever, cough, runny nose, red eyes, and sore throat. Two or three days after symptoms begin, tiny white spots (Koplik's spots) may appear inside the mouth. Three to five days after the start of symptoms, a red or reddish-brown rash appears. The rash usually begins on a person's face at the hairline and spreads downward to the neck, trunk, arms, legs, and feet. When the rash appears, a person's fever may spike to more than 104 degrees Fahrenheit. After a few days, the fever subsides and the rash fades." (A fever is a body's way of fighting disease.)

All of my children had chickenpox. Yes, they were miserable for several days, but they survived. They have all had the flu and have healed from it. I believe we do what doctors tell us to do way too easily without researching exactly what is in the vaccinations and what the long-term side effects are. Now adults are getting chickenpox which is WAY more dangerous than children getting it, and when you get a certain strain of the flu, chickenpox or measles, your body develops a natural immunity to them so you will never get them again.

My grandmother had seven children. She was born in the very early 1900s way before any studies on vaccinations had been done. She birthed all of her children in her home and didn't vaccinate any of them. She didn't want to put that "poison" into their bodies as she put it. She raised them on a lot of fruits and vegetables, meat, dairy, and eggs. She always had a large garden. Only one of the seven got cancer and that was the oldest son. He smoked and got lung cancer. All five daughters have lived at least until their late 80s. My mom was diagnosed with cancer when she was 80 as I have already written about.

I am not telling you to vaccinate or not to vaccinate but do a lot of research before you put any vaccine or drug into your body. All drugs and vaccinations have side effects. Most healthy bodies can fight most diseases. I believe a healthy immune system is the key to good health. There is just too much autism, autoimmune diseases, and cancer to not cause us to be leery of adding one more toxin to our children's bodies. Be a wise parent and make decisions carefully, prayerfully, and with a lot of research.

"If any of you lacks wisdom, let him ask God,
who gives generously to all without reproach,
and it will be given to him" James 1:5.

MOTHERS LEAVING HOME CONTRIBUTED TO THE FATTENING OF AMERICA

There are always new reasons I am figuring out how women leaving their homes and getting careers has harmed our society. When mothers left their homes for careers, fast food became the norm. Mothers were no longer around to shop for nutritious food and then prepare it. Mothers were no longer around to be at parks or in the neighborhoods to watch the children play outside. Families began relying on fast food, processed and packaged food, and junk food. Children began eating poorly and exercising less. They came home to empty homes and entertained themselves by eating junk food and watching junk television. Families stopped having family dinners together. Thus, children became overweight.

When my children were very young, I drove a half hour to a healthy food store to buy nutritious food for my family. I spent a lot of time in the kitchen preparing healthy food for them. Every afternoon, I would go into the cul-de-sac and watch them play outside with all the neighborhood children when they were young. If they weren't in the cul-de-sac, they were in the backyard playing. I wouldn't allow them to come home, eat junk food, and watch television when they were older. I was there, guarding and watching over my family and home.

Was I perfect? No, and I hope I never come across that way, but I was home taking care of my family where I believe mothers should be. Running a home and taking care of a family takes a lot of time and energy. It is absolutely a full-time job. We should have never left this very important job for others to do; others who don't care about our family's health. We gave away our family's health to big corporations who use the lowest quality food, including chemicals not designed for human consumption and were only in it for the money.

Mothers, come home to your family. Begin watching over and guarding your home. Take time to fix nutritious food, watch your children play outside, and read to them. Tell them all the wonderful Bible stories of old and about the Rock of the Ages. You were created to be at home with your children. They need you.

"She opens her mouth with wisdom, and the teaching of kindness is on her tongue. She looks well to the ways of her household and does not eat the bread of idleness" (Proverbs 31:26,27).

DANGERS OF ANTIDEPRESSANTS

Dr. Oz had a show on the dangers of antidepressants. Someone very close to me was put on them many years ago due to heart palpitations and anxiety. She has tried weaning herself off of them for many years and has had a horrible time of it. These drugs have literally stolen her life.

Years ago when I was in a lot of pain, I took a strong painkiller for a while. Little did I know that it had an anti-depressant in it. The reason I have been able to make it through the past 25 years in pain was due to having a strong mind. I am able to renew my mind with God's truth and reason myself through the pain.

While on that drug, I lost the ability to do that, and it was horrible. It took me two weeks after stopping taking it to rid myself of the withdrawal symptoms. I have decided I would rather live in pain instead of on pain killers and all the side effects that come with it.

I wouldn't be surprised if most, if not all, of the mass murders in the past ten years have been committed by men who were on antidepressants. There has probably been a steep rise in suicides also since one of the side effects is suicide.

Dr. Oz said that many women are on antidepressants now. It is becoming more and more common. If I was ever diagnosed with depression, I would do many things before I would even think about taking an antidepressant. One Christian psychologist shared with us years ago that when he began his practice 50 years ago, the average age of onset depression was 45-year-old women. He predicted back then that in 10 years, one out of four teenagers would be on antidepressants. I wouldn't be surprised if he was right.

Change your diet dramatically to a healthy diet without chemicals in it. Eat more sun-dried salt like Redmond's salt which has more than 80 different micronutrients. Get out in the sunshine a lot and exercise. Read the Bible more and listen to the news less or maybe not at all.

Before you take any drugs or have them given to your children, study them carefully and all the side effects. Then make an informed decision whether taking the drug is worth the risk. I realize depression is a horrible illness to bear but consider carefully your route for trying to get well. The drug route may make you worse.

"For God has not given us the spirit of fear; but of power, and of love, and of a sound mind." (2 Timothy 1:7)

THE SECRET TO LOSING WEIGHT

Eat less. Move more. That is it. There is no secret. I read a few years ago that Trisha Yearwood lost thirty pounds and said this was her secret. For her, it is a battle every day to not eat that cookie and she is usually slightly hungry.

Years ago, my parents met with three other couples that they have been friends with since they were young. My dad told me that out of the four couples, one was thin and in shape. The rest were twenty to thirty pounds overweight. They were all in their eighties, but this thin couple looked ten years younger than the rest. They go to the gym five days a week and eat in moderation. This greatly impressed him!

My dad gets a ton of health magazines and preaches the benefits of antioxidants and being in shape, yet he struggles to lose weight. He knows he should but it is so difficult once you put on the weight.

It is being said that this generation will not live longer than previous generations because of being overweight. It is a serious problem that leads to many diseases.

I know it is difficult to lose weight. I think the only reason I stay so thin is from two brain surgeries and a neck fusion with feeling poorly most of the time. It affects my stomach, so I am not that hungry. Whenever I go through times when I feel well, I have to battle my appetite and my weight so I know it isn't easy.

So I don't have a secret to losing weight, except I would encourage you to give up sugar completely if you can since it is so addictive and destructive to your health. Don't let that cookie or piece of cake control and master you. You master it! I would also encourage you to just eat as healthy as you can and exercise as much as you can.

We are commanded to be known for our moderation, and gluttony is a sin. We are told we can do all things through Christ who strengthens us. We have everything we need for life and godliness, including self-control. Now, start believing God's many promises and act upon them.

"Let your moderation be known unto all men. The Lord is at hand." (Philippians 4:5)

DOES CHOLESTEROL CAUSE HEART DISEASE?

Apparently not, believes two doctors that were on the Dr. Oz show. (I used to watch his show years ago!) One of them had been a cardiologist for many years and said that half of his patients have high cholesterol and no heart disease while the other half of his patients have low cholesterol with heart disease.

He said the side effects of statin drugs can be diabetes, cancer, and other dangerous diseases and are detrimental to one's health. He believes the main cause of heart disease is inflammation in the body.

He fervently believes that neither cholesterol nor fat is the major villain in the American diet – sugar and seed oils are. He also believes that the case against cholesterol, which was made nearly 30 years ago, was based on faulty evidence. The case needs to be re-opened and the evidence needs to be re-examined.

They believe grass-fed beef is very good for you because it has omega-3s in it, while regular beef is harmful since it is loaded with hormones, pesticides, and antibiotics. Dr. Marshall also taught that statin drugs rob the body of CoQ10 which is vital to having a healthy heart.

We were visiting one of my mom's friend's years on a road trip. He was in constant pain from the waist down and could hardly walk. He said it was from taking statin drugs for many years.

In conclusion, stop eating sugar and seed oils and anything with these in them, especially if you are experiencing health problems.

You may be thinking, "What does she know about health? She has a brain tumor?" Every single one of my blood tests, x-rays, EKG, etc. are normal. All of my organs and blood are healthy. My doctor said to me, "Who knows where you would be now if you didn't take such good care of yourself?" I believe my tumor is from the trauma of running into a sliding glass door full speed, being thrown back onto my back, and breaking my nose in three places when I was younger, not from eating unhealthy food!

We live in a very fallen world, as you all know, and cannot control everything that happens to us. We must do our best and leave the rest in the Lord's hands.

Inflammation in the body causes cancer, diabetes, and many of the diseases we suffer from today. Start being careful what you eat. Read labels and fix most of your own food without chemicals and preservatives. It takes time, but good health is worth it.

"An intelligent heart acquires knowledge, and the ear of the wise seeks knowledge." (Proverbs 18:15)

FIGHTING INFECTIONS WITHOUT DRUGS

Doctors fight infections with antibiotics. My grandmother, who raised seven children, fought infections with lemon and honey water. She believed God gave us immune systems to fight infections. I much prefer her way. There are no side effects!

When one of my daughters was young, she had quite a few ear infections. I went the medical route for a while. She would get an ear infection, and the doctor would put her on an antibiotic. I finally read Dr. Mendelsohn's book. He was a pediatrician for over 30 years and said the children with ear infections who took antibiotics got well just as quickly as those who didn't take any. The only difference was that the ones who didn't take antibiotics didn't continue getting ear infections. Antibiotics weaken the immune system.

Our bodies have an amazing ability to develop immunities. I finally allowed her own body to heal her ear infections, and she no longer got ear infections. Dr. Mendolsohn recommends that as soon as an infection begins, get off all sugar and eat pure, good food.

Several years ago, I got a bladder infection. It was extremely painful. I was even bleeding from it. I did not want to go on antibiotics, however. My gut is so sensitive from all the drugs I took trying to get rid of the parasites years ago. I had my husband get me some organic cranberry juice from the health food store. I lived on that, lemon and honey water, and lots of vitamin C. Within several days, I was much better. Clear Tract is an excellent thing to take for UTIs and bladder infections too. I found this cleared them up in a couple of days!

After one of my babies, I got mastitis where the breast gets infected shortly after birth. It was also very painful. I kept warm heat on my breast and drank lots of lemon and honey water along with other fresh juices. Within several days, I was fine. Allow the fever to fight off the infection!

Our bodies do an amazing job at healing themselves if given the right fuel. I loved having Dr. Mendelsohn's book so I could know if something truly was an emergency or not. If it was an emergency, we definitely took our children to the doctor but most of the time, it was not an emergency and I just let my children's body do the healing.

Beware of taking antibiotics. They are way over prescribed now and lead to all sorts of diseases, I believe. My dad and close friend almost died from an antibiotic. I want to remind you that I am not a doctor. This is just my opinion so take it as such!

LEMON AND HONEY WATER

Warm up a cup of water, not boiling.

Put in a teaspoon or more of raw, organic honey and stir.

Add the juice of a whole lemon.

You don't want the water too warm or it will kill the vitamin C in the lemon juice.

*"I praise you because I am fearfully and
wonderfully made; your works are wonderful; I know that full well." (Psalm 139:14)*

LET FOOD BE YOUR MEDICINE

Did you know that eating out can be hazardous to your
health? Now, I know you can't control everything in life and
there should be good times but we must be knowledgeable,
not living our lives blindly. Practically all restaurants cook all
of their food in seed oils which are dangerous to our health,
as I have already written about.

Our family used to get some food from Oscars (a restaurant
here in San Diego) frequently. Most of us had stomach aches
after eating their food. I finally read the ingredients on their
salad dressing. It was filled with chemicals that should not be
eaten. I am sure most of their food contained cheap, artificial
ingredients. This restaurant eventually went out of business.

The Food Babe gave a detailed description of the ingredients from different foods at Panera. There were some toxic
chemicals in many of their foods, and it is supposed to be
a "healthier" alternative.

Dr. Marshall always said on his radio program that eating
out is playing Russian Roulette with your health. You have
no idea what is in the food, and restaurants usually cut a
lot of corners by using bad chemicals and preservatives in
their food. I almost always eat at home.

Cancer, heart disease, diabetes, and autoimmune diseases
are skyrocketing, and this has been since seed oils hit the
market. The news recently reported that half of all men will
get cancer and a third of all women. There are many things

you can do to help prevent cancer and these other diseases. The most important thing you can do is to stay away from all types of toxic chemicals.

Kraft Macaroni and Cheese has two artificial dyes added to it which contain petroleum in them. Europe is not allowed to use these chemicals, so they use food sources to dye their food. Their Krapf Macaroni and Cheese is dyed with some herbs and tastes just as good. America uses chemicals, because they are cheaper.

So go ahead and eat out once in a while, but make most of your food at home using good, organic ingredients. Know what it is in your food. Hippocrates is considered the father of Western Medicine. Some of his wise advice included, "Let food be thy medicine and let thy medicine be food."

Eat food the way God intended for us to eat. Anything boxed or canned is processed and is usually bad for your health. Health is a terrible thing to lose. I know. Protect your health. Be wise in what you put into your body. Begin diligently reading labels!

"Behold, I send you forth as sheep in the midst of wolves: be ye therefore wise as serpents, and harmless as doves." (Matthew 10:16)

YOU NEED SUNSHINE!

Have you noticed that the flu hits in the dead of winter? Colds are prevalent then also. They are discovering that it is due to a lack of Vitamin D. The best way to get Vitamin D is from the sun; imagine that! They keep discovering what God made is the best for us.

One woman told me about her two grandmothers. One never went in the sun, had beautiful skin, but always struggled with ill health. Her other grandmother was always outside in the sun, had wrinkled skin, but was full of vitality and good health.

Florence Nightingale is known for saying that the patients who were on the southern side of the hospital building, which is full of sunlight, got well while those on the northern side did not. When looking for a home, I always looked for a sunny one with a western or southern exposure. I always keep all my window coverings open during the day to allow the sun to permeate my home.

When my mom had colitis and went to health resorts, they always had the sick people sit in the sun for an hour a day in the morning or afternoon. Whenever my children were sick, I would encourage them to go in the backyard and sit in the sun. I never encouraged sunscreen. I just don't trust putting a bunch of chemicals on your skin. Now, whenever I have a sore on my skin that doesn't heal, I use Black Salve, and it works great!!

Do what you can to stay healthy and leave the rest in God's hands.

*"Your word is a lamp to my feet and a
light to my path." (Psalm 119:105)*

ARE DRUGS MAKING US HEALTHIER?

Few people recognize that natural infections, especially early in life, can actually be beneficial as they serve to build a very strong and resilient immune system for later life. In the days before vaccination, people's immune systems were allowed to become strong in such a way. This means that, as they aged, people in previous generations were significantly stronger and less likely to die of disease than today.

When I was growing up, I can't remember anyone with allergies, asthma, or autism. Some women had breast cancer, but it wasn't nearly as prevalent as it is today. America has become a pill-popping society; falsely believing that drugs will keep them healthy. Did you know that one of the first things doctors learn in medical school is that ALL drugs are toxic to the human body and should be given as a last resort after trying diet and lifestyle changes first?

Children are given close to 49 vaccinations before they turn six years old! People are so afraid of getting sick that they allow themselves to be injected with substances they have no idea how their bodies will react to or what the long-term consequences will be.

Drugs don't cure. They are great for emergency situations but not to cure disease. God gave us amazing immune systems to heal and fight disease. Our older population is not healthy. Most of them are taking fistfuls of drugs daily and burdening our overly burdened health care.

It has been noted that there are a growing number of people living in their 100s, implying modern life is healthy. Yet, we must remember these people were mostly living in rural areas and small villages where life was hard, diets were mostly natural, and modern medicines were rarely used until the extremes of age. It is our early years which determine how healthy we will live in our later years. Their early life was during a time when most modern medicine and pesticides didn't exist.

These are people who were minimally vaccinated, ate better diets, mostly avoided medicine until absolutely needed, had strong family and social bonds, and worked very hard all their lives.

Drugs and chemicals play havoc on your digestive health. They destroy the friendly flora that keeps you healthy. Here are a few recommendations to staying healthy in a toxic environment:

1. Take a lot of good probiotics: kefir, kombucha, sauerkraut, etc.

2. Stay as far away from plastics and chemicals as you can.

3. Clean with non-toxic cleaners

4. Eat as organically as you can afford.

5. Get fresh air, sunshine, and exercise.

6. Only use drugs when absolutely needed.

"Therefore, since we have these promises, dear friends, let us purify ourselves from everything that contaminates body and spirit, perfecting holiness out of reverence for God." (2 Corinthians 7:1)

HOW TO AVOID THE FLU

The following recommendations are taken from Dr. Mercola's website. It is such good information that I thought all of you should read it given the hysteria the media has over the flu every season and the mass marketing of the flu shot and now the Covid shot. I was with two pharmacists' friends a few years ago and they both said they would never get either shot. Something to think about.

Your Gut Flora. This may be the single most important strategy you can implement as the bacteria in your gut have enormous control of your immune response. The best way to improve your beneficial bacteria ratio is to avoid sugars as they will feed the pathogenic bacteria. Additionally, processed foods and most grains should be limited and replaced with healthy fats like coconut oil, avocados, olives, olive oil, butter, eggs, and nuts. Once you change your diet, then regular use of fermented foods can radically optimize the function of your immune response.

Optimize your vitamin D levels. As I've previously reported, optimizing your vitamin D levels is one of the absolute best strategies for avoiding infections of ALL kinds, and vitamin D deficiency may actually be the true culprit behind the seasonality of the flu – not the flu virus itself. This is probably the single most important and least expensive action you can take. Regularly monitor your vitamin D levels to confirm your levels are within the therapeutic range of 50-70 ng/ml.

Ideally, you'll want to get all your vitamin D from sun exposure or a safe tanning bed, but as a last resort you can take an oral vitamin D3 supplement. According to the latest review by Carole Baggerly (Grassrootshealth.org), adults need about 8,000 IU's a day. Be sure to take vitamin K2 if you are taking high dose oral vitamin D as it has a powerful synergy and will help prevent any D toxicity.

Avoid Sugar and Processed Foods. Sugar impairs the quality of your immune response almost immediately, and as you likely know, a healthy immune system is one of the most important keys to fighting off viruses and other illnesses. It also can decimate your beneficial bacteria and feed the pathogenic yeast and viruses. Be aware that sugar (typically in the form of high fructose corn syrup) is present in foods you may not suspect, like ketchup and fruit juice. If you are healthy then sugar can be consumed, but the LAST thing you should be eating when you are sick is sugar. Avoid it like poison while you are sick.

Get Plenty of Rest. Just like it becomes harder for you to get your daily tasks done if you're tired, if your body is overly fatigued it will be harder for it to fight the flu. Be sure to check out my article "Guide to a Good Night's Sleep" for some great tips to help you get quality rest.

Have Effective Tools to Address Stress. We all face some stress every day, but if stress becomes overwhelming then your body will be less able to fight off the flu and other illnesses. My solution to stress, Lori writing here, is to take every thought captive to the obedience of Christ. Renew your mind daily with God's Word. Dwell on the good and the lovely. Remind yourself daily that the joy of the LORD is your strength, God's grace is sufficient, and you can do all things through Christ who strengthens you. The battle is in the mind. Remember, God promises us a sound mind. Believe Him!

Get Regular Exercise. When you exercise, you increase your circulation and your blood flow throughout your body. The components of your immune system are also better circulated, which means your immune system has a better chance of fighting an illness before it spreads. Be sure to stay hydrated – drink plenty of fluids, especially water. However, it would be wise to radically reduce the intensity of your workouts while you are sick. No Peak Fitness exercises until you are better.

Take a High-Quality Source of Animal-Based Omega-3 Fats. Increase your intake of healthy and essential fats like the omega-3 found in krill oil, which is crucial for maintaining health. It is also vitally important to avoid damaged omega-6 oils that are trans fats and in processed foods as it will seriously damage your immune response. (Sardines and grass fed beef are the best foods for this in my opinion!)

Wash Your Hands. Washing your hands will decrease your likelihood of spreading a virus to your nose, mouth or other people. Be sure you don't use antibacterial soap for this – antibacterial soaps are completely unnecessary, and they cause far more harm than good. Instead, identify a simple chemical-free soap that you can have your family use.

Tried and True Hygiene Measures. In addition to washing your hands regularly, cover your mouth and nose when you cough or sneeze. If possible, avoid close contact with those who are sick and, if you are sick, avoid close contact with those who are well.

Use Natural Antibiotics. Examples include oil of oregano and garlic. These work like broad-spectrum antibiotics against bacteria, viruses, and protozoa in your body. And unlike pharmaceutical antibiotics, they do not appear to lead to resistance. (X-Clear is fantastic at preventing all respiratory illnesses.)

Avoid Hospitals. I'd recommend you stay away from hospitals unless you're having an emergency and need expert medical care, as hospitals are prime breeding grounds for infections of all kinds. The best place to get plenty of rest and recover from illness that is not life-threatening is usually in the comfort of your own home. (There is NO place like home!)

THE HEART OF THE HOME

Written By Lisa Vitello in her long ago newsletter New Harvest Homestead

> I love old-fashioned things (big surprise, right?). Within the space of a few years, both of my grandmothers decided to move out of their long-time homes and into retirement communities. They each generously offered to let me have anything

from their kitchens that I wanted.

I had struck the mother lode.

Cast iron Dutch ovens and frying pans, seasoned and blackened with use, milk glass butter dishes and nesting hens, and Pyrex primary color bowls. I was in heaven.

One of the treasures I now possess from those happy days is the 1950 edition of the Betty Crocker cookbook. As I perused the fragile, yellowing pages, I came across this heart-warming sentiment in the introduction:

"[This cookbook] is dedicated to homemakers everywhere – to all who like to minister to dear ones by serving them good food."

These words both touched my heart and caused a pang of sadness at the same time. I can't imagine a modern, mass market cookbook containing this type of language. They might get sued or something! And, I don't know a lot of women who truly regard their efforts in the kitchen as a ministry. But that is what it can be if we approach it that way. Instead of looking upon the preparation of food as a burden or nuisance, what if we could see it as a holy calling, as important as any other ministry to which Christians are called? That might just change our entire countenance, don't you think?

Food is an integral part of all of our lives. We mark the most important occasions with a meal, whether it be a wedding, a holiday, the birth of a child, or even in death. A meal shared together is one of the most intimate forms of human communion.

The night before Jesus was to suffer and die on the cross, He shared a Passover meal with His disciples. He said,

"I have earnestly desired to eat this Passover with

you before I suffer..." (Luke 22:15). This wonderful Savior wanted nothing more on the night before His agonizing death than to share a quiet meal with His best friends. I wonder if those who prepared the meal understood how much it meant to Him; that it truly ministered to Him.

There are so many references in the Word of God to feasts and meals, one could write an entire book on the subject (I'm sure many have). The holiest of days are celebrated with feasts. The first Christians shared meals together as a regular part of their fellowship, and our future union with the Lord in the kingdom of heaven will be inaugurated with a joyful wedding feast. In fact, Jesus said that He Himself will serve that meal to His beloved ones on that awesome day (See Luke 12:37). I can't wait to taste that food!

So, this whole matter of preparing and serving food is no small thing to the Lord, and neither should it be for us. If the King of kings would stoop to serve the lowliest of the low with loving care, then we have no business grumbling and groaning that this humble task has fallen upon our shoulders as wives and mothers. Colossians 3:23 states:

"Whatever you do, do your work heartily, as for the Lord rather than for men; knowing that from the Lord you will receive the reward of the inheritance. It is the Lord Christ whom you serve."

I like that word "heartily" – meaning with your whole heart. When we approach our everyday obligations with that attitude, we are promised to reap a reward in heaven, as much as if we had served the Master Himself. The list of good works worthy of the kingdom of heaven in Matthew 25 does not include any incredible feats, but rather the commonplace acts of giving someone something to eat and drink or visiting the sick. Jesus said inasmuch as we do these things to the "least," we have done so for Him. Do we not consider our families much more highly than the "least?"

What does a good, home-cooked meal say to our husbands? To his mind it says, "I love you. I appreciate how hard you work. You deserve this." When we take the time and care to prepare really nourishing, delicious snacks and meals for our children, we are telling them that their well-being is paramount in our minds. We want them to grow strong and healthy. This is indeed a ministry of love. The woman of the house, more than any other member, will be responsible for drawing her family together around the dinner table on a regular basis. This is about much more than just eating; it is about sharing ourselves with one another.

The kitchen is the place where a lot of us will spend the better part of our days – especially when we have embraced the "homestead" lifestyle. Let's be like that good lady in Proverbs 31 and work with our hands in delight to bless our families, our neighbors, and all whom the Lord will bring to our door.

MY KITCHEN PRAYER

God bless my little kitchen,
I love its every nook,
And bless me as I do my work,
Wash pots and pans and cook.
And may the meals that I prepare
Be seasoned from above
With Thy great blessing
And Thy grace
But, most of all, Thy love.

***My favorite thing in life to do is to gather around a table and enjoy a meal together with family, friends, and neighbors. These times add so much richness to my life! I look forward to the great wedding feast we will all have together one day with Jesus Christ. Oh, what a day that will be!

WHERE I BUY MY FOOD

Eating organic, healthy food is expensive, but it's worth it for your health. I decided to make a list for you of what I buy and where I buy it to help you better figure out how to afford as much as you can. It's far better to give up some luxuries in your life so you can eat healthier. Cancer, heart disease, and diabetes are extremely expensive. It's far better to do what you can to prevent these horrible diseases.

These are the items I buy from Costco which has a lot of organic food and everything I buy there is organic unless specified:

- Frozen blueberries
- Sauerkraut
- Lemons (not organic)
- Avocados (not organic)
- Cucumbers
- Peppers
- Mushrooms
- Frozen green beans and peas
- Butter
- Extra virgin olive oil (not organic is better than organic!)
- Avocado oil
- Whole chickens
- Ground turkey

- Ground beef
- Walnuts
- Canned tomato sauce
- Tomato paste
- Coconut oil
- Sardines
- Wild caught salmon in cans
- Avocado Mayonnaise
- Maple Syrup

These are what I buy from my local health food store. When we're in Wisconsin, I buy all of my meat, eggs, fruit, and vegetables from a local farm. Farmer's Markets are great too!

- Lettuce (Romaine, Red Leaf, and Arugula)
- Carrots
- Radicchio
- Onions
- Garlic
- Zucchini
- Broccoli
- Green beans
- Spaghetti squash
- Fruit in season
- Potatoes
- Yams
- Tomatoes
- Bananas
- Pastured, organic eggs
- Steaks
- Ground beef
- Turkey
- Raw, organic cheese

(I just shop the exterior of the health food store and buy all of the interior things online since they're a lot cheaper.)

This is what I buy from Vitacost online when they have a sale for 15 to 20 percent off (sign up for their texts):

- Einkorn flour in 10 pound bags

This is what I buy from Thrive Market online (all organic):
- Coconut sugar
- Coconut milk
- Peanut Butter
- Ketchup
- Redmond's Real Salt
- Acure Shampoo
- Hand Soap
- Mini-chocolate chips
- Sprouted pumpkin seeds
- Giovanni Hair Spritz (Hairspray)
- Dr. Bronner's Sal Suds (Dish soap)
- Ghee
- Canned Pumpkin (Costco has it in the Fall)
- Balsamic Vinegar
- Pickles
- Pasta
- Sprouted Brown Rice Flour (for sourdough bread)
- Classic Marinara Sauce
- Raw Honey (Local if you can find it!)
- Beef Tallow

My Closing
Encouragement
To You

*D*ear women who have read the entirety of this book, I hope I haven't discouraged you. If you have never heard these things, it sounds overwhelming to you. Just begin with baby steps. When you run out of your laundry detergent, switch to a non-toxic version. Begin shopping the exterior of the supermarket. Try one recipe a month. Cut up some vegetables and dip them in the salad dressing I shared. Try cutting out sugar for a week. Get out and walk for 10 minutes a day. Maybe go to bed an hour earlier. It's a good thing to discipline ourselves in all things! It's not easy, and this is why I recommend that you go slowly.

I was raised this way, so it's easy for me. I have also had many health problems since I was 30 years old, so I am always researching and trying ways to become healthier without drugs and doctors. Yes, I still need them, but they are my last resort.

Remember, we can only control what we can control. We can't control what's going on in our world, but we can control how we live our lives and care for our homes and families. Take control of what you can control and simply do the best you can do for today. Finances may be a problem. Do the best you can. Junk food is expensive and detrimental to your health. Health is a wonderful gift to have, and we should do all we can to give this gift to our families as much as it depends upon us.

My dad was a doctor his entire life. He once said that those with chronic health problems usually end up to be the healthiest since they research and take care of their health far more than others. I have found this to be true. Since I have had so many health problems, I do what I can to stay as healthy as possible and leave the rest in the Lord's hands. He has numbered our days. We can trust Him. He loves us. He is good, and His plan for us is good (Romans 8:28).

I must end this book with two of my favorite verses in which I try to build my life upon:

"I beseech you therefore, brethren, by the mercies of God, that ye present your bodies a living sacrifice, holy, acceptable unto God, which is your reasonable service. And be not conformed to this world: but be ye transformed by the renewing of your mind, that ye may prove what is that good, and acceptable, and perfect, will of God." (Romans 12:1,2)

ABOUT THE AUTHOR

Lori Alexander is a wife of 43 years and a mother of four grown, married children and eighteen grandchildren (two are still in the womb at this writing). She loves to mentor women in all of the ways of biblical womanhood. She began a blog "Always Learning" in 2011 after mentoring women since 2003. She's always loved teaching and found her calling after reading Debi Pearl's book "Created to Be His Help Meet." She then began her new blog "The Transformed Wife" in 2016 after publishing her first book "The Power of a Transformed Wife."

OTHER BOOKS BY LORI ALEXANDER

The Power of a Transformed Wife
Biblical Womanhood: A Study Guide
Daily Wisdom for Biblical Womanhood